SPRINT

— TO THE —

MOUNTAINTOP

SPRINT

— TO THE —

MOUNTAINTOP

How to Accelerate Your Journey to
Success with Unbridled Resolve

COLONEL MARK E. TATE, USAF (Ret.)

CONTENTS

INTRODUCTION

"Nothing good ever comes easy."

-Unknown

Through all the ups and downs of my college experience at Auburn University, I always knew I wanted to be an Air Force officer. Although I wasn't on a military scholarship, I joined the Reserve Officer Training Corps (ROTC) during my freshman year. I wasn't the best cadet, but I performed barely better than others and was able to get through ROTC with the help of some amazing Non-Commissioned Officers (NCOs) who offered me encouragement and the occasional odd job when I needed a few extra dollars to make ends meet.

It would take five-and-a-half years, but one Wednesday morning in August, I graduated with my degree. Later that day, I proudly raised my right hand as I took my commissioning oath of office. At that time, I vowed silently to myself that I would make the very best of this incredible opportunity to realize my lifelong dream of becoming an Air Force officer. The years I spent at Auburn grinding it out prepared me for just about anything life was going to throw my way.

I knew I needed to hit the ground running at my first duty assignment. My success depended on figuring out a way to effectively solve problems, communicate well, and get as much leadership training as I could along the way. My first assignment was certainly not for anyone wishing to remain close to home. I was sent over 7,900 miles away to Guam for an overseas short tour lasting 15 months. The short tour was a blessing in disguise because the experiences on Guam taught me amazing lessons in friendship, collaboration, leadership, accountability, integrity, and hard work. That assignment laid the foundation of my future success.

Nearly two years ago, I retired as a colonel from the Air Force after serving over 27 years as a logistician. During the course of my service at 17 different duty assignments across the world, I picked up quite a few lessons. I thrived in multiple situations during both regular and wartime operations while working with many people from diverse military and civilian backgrounds. The operations tempo for many positions was intense, and the complexity of the problems we solved was mind numbing. The projects I worked on were impactful at the tactical, operational, and strategic levels. Now, I want to share my experiences so others can learn how to confidently take on a new role or challenge and overcome a steep learning curve in far less time than ever before.

Why This Book is Important to You

This book is for anyone working in a highly demanding job who is struggling to attain the tools and techniques needed to overcome leadership or occupational challenges and wants to fuel the upward trajectory of their career to reach new heights in far less time. In this book, I have distilled the methods I used to successfully lead organizations, work with highly talented people, manage resources, and collaborate with stakeholders to solve difficult problems. Many times, it seemed that the clock was quickly ticking. The problems I faced needed expedited solutions or at least multiple options or courses of action to pass along to more senior leaders.

Critical thinking and complex problem solving takes training and experience. In the course of my career, I have found that, many times, it takes a significant number of months for people to gain their professional footing whenever they start working at a new organization, get promoted, transferred, or take on a challenging responsibility. On average, it takes someone about ten months until they are comfortable with tackling any challenge, are impactful, and can be relied on as the subject matter expert. I call this time of learning and growing in the organization the tumultuous ten. Those ten months are spent getting oriented, figuring out what right looks like, and grinding it out with long hours of putting in the work.

Early in my career, I noticed that I was only keeping pace, and it really frustrated me. I knew I needed to be one or more steps ahead of my peers. I was unsure why it was taking me so long to get up to speed. Then, I started being very deliberate about my plan for success. I started to compress the time it took me to get fully engaged and make contributions to the team.

Overcoming the woes of the tumultuous ten significantly reduces the amount of time you need to learn and grow before you become a difference maker in your organization. It does not matter if you have been in your industry for one month or many years; the techniques in this book can help you. There's no such thing as being done with learning, so if you have the desire to be better, then this book is for you.

Starting any endeavor can be stressful. There's the internal and external pressure of wanting to produce, contribute, and win. If you have a range of tools to deal with challenges, you will be less stressed; therefore, you will make better decisions. You will soon arrive at a point where you are skilled in identifying gaps and seams and building plans to mitigate potential problems. As you become comfortable with your growth, you will also recognize and embrace the merits of collaboration, feedback, and self reflection. Now, I want to share with you the knowledge that I've picked up over the years so you can learn to accelerate your career and life into high gear to achieve the success you deserve.

The Potential Outcome

Imagine waking up in the morning before you begin your work with a clear understanding of the major tasks for the day. You have a sense of peace because you know what levers to pull throughout the day if you encounter tough problems. The burdens of a typical day are very manageable, and instead of finishing your day stumbling across the finish line at the end of the day, you finish the day with a sprint, and you aren't even winded.

If you embrace the ideas of the book, you will become an invaluable member of your team. You will gain a reputation as a key asset to the organization, and as a result, you will gain the respect and admiration of higher level leaders and peers. Respect won't come from sheer luck; it will be because you're a recognized subject matter expert who understands the importance of paying attention to the details. Your productivity and efficiency will be off the charts, and you will likely get tapped for additional opportunities in the organization.

If You Don't Act Now

Sometimes, we hesitate because we think about how sloppy things look as we attempt to do something for the first time. Sure, it will probably be a bit rough, but once you slosh through the transition period, things will get remarkably better. Dancing like no one is looking probably isn't on anyone's list of things to do, but if we get in our own head too much, paralysis by analysis will certainly happen. So, you must be keenly aware that this book is about growing and pushing through the current limits that are likely self imposed.

If you don't push yourself, there is a strong chance that you will have the proverbial conversation with yourself in a few weeks that starts with, "I plan to do this tomorrow or at a more opportune time when life is less busy." Well, for many of us, that train has already left the station. We are incredibly busy with all the good and bad that life throws our way every day.

The number one reason for reading this book and adopting these tools and techniques is that your mental and physical health can probably benefit. Having a plan that lays the foundation for future success is what helped me get through some pretty tough times. Sometimes, just knowing that you are moving towards a goal is helpful.

If you don't make the decision to move forward with the concepts of this book, you will be in constant search for the ideal job that meets all your expectations. The unfortunate reality is that you will never find that number one, super job that's being held indefinitely by human resources for you. You won't ever find the dream job because you will never give your absolute best effort in any position. You will always have an excuse for your lackluster performance and move on to the next job, instead of really digging in and focusing on being the best version of yourself each day.

Over the course of time, bitterness will set in, and you will find yourself angry at others because "it" will always be someone's fault. You will say things like, "Geez, those people should have promoted me years ago," "No one ever recognized my hard work," or "Those people aren't right. You have to be a snake to earn a seat at their table." Friends, let's get ready to put in some work now to prevent any of these negative thoughts or ideas from creeping into your mind. I'm looking forward to sharing the wonderful view from the mountaintop as you take the path to achieve your destiny. I'll see you at the top!

CHAPTER 1

Being Barely Better Than Others (3BTO) Won't Get You Ahead

"Life is short. Don't do the same thing everyone else is doing – that's such a herd mentality. And don't do something that's two percent better than the other person. Do something that changes the world."

– Oren Etzioni

When it comes time to really lean forward and put in the immense effort needed to reach our goals, we start out strong. However, in more cases than we dare care to admit, our commitment soon goes from being at an astronomical height to barely hovering above rock bottom. Soon, the bell tolls for our lost, broken dream. We file the experience as a far-fetched goal that we couldn't have achieved anyway.

Our hope is replaced by something different altogether as we become overwhelmed and unsure of our future. That replacement is mediocracy. For a while, we default to the old standby of being just a little bit better than the competition. You see, anyone can start out strong on their mission and end up getting caught up in the maelstrom of mediocrity.

After reading this chapter, you will be ready to shake off the shackles of being an average person and rip off whatever weights are holding you back from reaching the summit of your dreams and aspirations. So, let's get going on our journey to overcome the tumultuous ten and achieve the greatness that you deserve.

The Siren's Song: Avoid the Enticement of Mediocracy

The heat from the hot tarmac smacked me in the face as soon as the cargo doors opened. I quickly gathered my gear, walked into the line, and started my measured descent down the ramp of the aircraft. I took a quick survey of the area around me. I had no idea how long I would be in my new location, but I knew that it would probably be at least 5 months.

Over the next few weeks, the people I arrived with quickly got into the routine of the deployment. Some even had countdown calendars that marked each day until they would take the freedom bird back home to civilization. All around me, people did their jobs, but they didn't really go above and beyond. You see, all the days consisted of pretty much doing the same things over and over again. It was like being on a movie set without the amenities. As with a lot of things in life, we default to the basics when faced with a different and difficult situation, especially when there appears to be no end in sight.

This deployment became my siren's song. Over the next few months, I slipped away and fell into the enticement of my own crappy experiences as a mediocre performer. It nearly led to my undoing. Over time, I realized my flaws and clawed my way back onto the right path for success. It took dedicated time and focused effort to get back on track. I hope you heed my advice so you won't make the same mistakes and have to fight so hard to get back on the path to your destiny.

Defining Being Barely Better Than Others (3BTO)

3BTO means doing *just* above the all-around bare minimum to maintain one's current position. There are no pockets of excellence or doing better in some areas than others. A 3BTO "practitioner" certainly is not the recipient of a deluge of kudos for a job well done. These folks do just a sliver above the basics of what is required to get the job done. In fact, some of them relish in the fact that they are able to "get over" by doing the least amount to earn their paycheck.

The trappings of a 3BTO teammate are fairly easy to identify, but it is sometimes hard to know if you have fallen into the trap yourself. The tell tale sign is when you look around and see that you and most people on your team are going through the motions. They are absolutely doing their jobs, but they are moving along with the enthusiasm and focus of an ant walking along a trail.

Their purpose becomes making it through another day so they can come back to work another day. You'll also be able to feel it when you walk into a room because few, if any, people are cheerful. In fact, if you show up with a smile instead of a frown, some may even think you're not living by the shared mantra, which is to avoid all work perceived as an extra duty. You'll also start making excuses for your level of performance, complain about the crap the last shift left you to do, and say *no* to pretty much everything.

If you're sinking into the trap, you will temper all ambition and live by the creed that all you have to do is screw up just a little less than the people around you. You will keep your head down and move forward, albeit in a zig-zag fashion with nary a desire to get onto the path of greatness. The long lasting effect is developing an uncanny knack at avoiding saying yes or providing exceptional customer service. In some ways, I think we have all experienced moments in life where 3BTO reared its ugly head and took its pound of flesh from us.

How the 3BTO Ideas Creep into Your Strategy and Goals

Initially, the allure of what 3BTO offers seems to make good sense, and you find yourself asking, "why not?" I mean, who wouldn't want to provide a bit less rigor in analysis, especially since it will likely change once your boss gets their hands on the document? You could have saved those extra three hours and worked on another tasker you were given days before that now waits to rise from the ashes of your inbox.

As the weeks pass, you take note of the landscape and begin the process of identifying everyone that has been caught in the 3BTO trap. It quickly becomes an acceptable thing once you see a person in a higher position getting caught in the web. You're in great company. Soon, your outlook slowly changes. You start changing your strategic approach for getting things done. Instead of starting on a project or task early, you begin to adopt the strategy that it takes five minutes to do if you only have five minutes. You even sideline some of your goals as being too ambitious to start and too much of a drain to finish; those goals are mentally placed in the graveyard of hopes and dreams. Heed these instructions: move swiftly across this barren landscape of zero future benefits and run onto the path of greatness with the speed of a cheetah.

Why the 3BTO Trap Limits Your Success

It's easy to figure out that adhering to the limit of being better than others will stunt your overall success. You must look at the impact to success across time and other future opportunities. Sometimes, the feeling of getting by with average performance may seem like a quick win today. Yes, it may give you some time to recover before the next big sprint, but what happens is that you lose your edge. It's just like a boxer who trains for a big fight, barely makes it to a draw, then takes eight months off from training. That person will have such a challenging time getting back into fighting trim that they may not ever be able to go back to being an elite athlete. It's the same way for us all in the workplace. We can't expect to coast along then just magically wake up one day back at the level of being an impact player.

Fools Gold: Why So Many People Fall Into the 3BTO Trap

When I was a kid, I grew up wanting to be a gold miner just like the people I read about in the history books. I remember digging in the woods with a friend one day when I unearthed a shiny rock about the size of my palm. I thought I had struck gold and was very excited to take it home to show my family. Imagine my dismay when my dad broke the news that I had unearthed nothing more than fools gold.

Just like the fools gold I found all those years ago, we sometimes fall into the 3BTO trap because it just seems to be a convenient option. We think of colleagues who we know weren't putting the work in but received accolades. We think, "Well, if they can do it and still achieve success, I surely can, too."

The problem with a copycat approach is twofold:

1. You don't know what the colleague is doing to succeed.
2. The colleague controls the narrative.

Why 3BTO Can Look Like a Good Option

It's a fact of life that we all can't be the best at everything we do. There are some people that will always be a bit better at one of those things you find difficult to do. Maybe it's because they work harder at perfecting their craft, or maybe it's because they figured out what it takes to win a bit sooner than you. I believe one thing that is consistent across the board. The one thing they do is very likely surround themselves with people and communities that are like minded. The people in their circles probably have the same ideals about what it takes to perform at a higher level than most.

If, instead, you are surrounded by people who are content with barely making it, you will probably be inclined to hitch your wagon to their thoughts and beliefs. So, your elders were right when they cautioned you about the people you hang out with. As adults, we can quickly lose sight and begin to swim in the sea of mediocrity. It's a fact that many of us lead busy, demanding lives that make it difficult to take time to survey the situation we are in and the people we keep company with. It's time to pause and take note of where you are right now in your professional and personal life.

In addition, you will also notice that 3BTO people operate in their own tribe. They always seem to know the latest techniques for skirting around a problem or situation. At times, it might even be at the expense of others. If you're thinking about joining them, resist the urge. Think about other options for a "friend" group because your personal success depends on you staying on track.

3BTO Dynamics that Derail Your Plans

Watching someone else quickly rise through the ranks within an elite organization in spite of their seemingly average performance can be a morale-shattering experience. Sometimes, we get so wrapped up in the success of others that we try to replicate the formula they created to achieve success. At first, you casually begin to doubt whatever plans you laid out to reach your success. Then, you're reminded that this person was only average yet is now at a higher level in the organization.

You go back to the drawing board with great haste to replan and retool. You spend time studying, trying to figure out how *that* person was able to fool everyone to reach the proverbial mountaintop. You make the mistake of making a hard stop on the plan you painstakingly created, and you unwisely pivot. I refer to this as the 3BTO dynamics that derail your plans.

You should realize that another person's success doesn't define your future success. It's just how the universe works. You can't have identical experiences or the unique opportunities that someone else had. More importantly, you can't always change your plans when you occasionally see oddities that come along with working around a person who makes it to higher positions in spite of their actual subpar performance. The path you charted was very likely a solid one, with the necessary tools you need to successfully get into the winner's circle. Don't let any of the noise from outside successes obscure your vivid vision of accomplishing your goals to achieve success.

3BTO Can Work for a While... Until You Fall Below the Standards

Have you ever been at the checkout line and remembered that you needed to buy batteries? You reluctantly get out of line and walk over to the battery display. There, you find the size batteries you need and are faced with a choice. You see the top tier choice that costs five dollars more than the cheaper alternative. Both are the right size, but the main difference is that the top tier batteries will likely last seven times longer than the bottom tier, cheaper alternative.

Just like the cheaper, bottom tier batteries, you can probably make it for a while being barely better than others. The outside packaging is the same, but the juice inside isn't. Over time, your energy erodes, and surprisingly, it takes more effort to be a few notches above average. You start missing suspenses to get taskers done. Then, one day, your boss calls you into the office to tell you that it's time for you to move on.

Crack the Code: Solve the 3BTO Dilemma

I remember my 3BTO dilemma even after all these years. I was four months into the deployment I mentioned earlier in the chapter. Those around me were still using their countdown charts but had steadily modified them as the deployment continued. The charts now included pictures of exotic, faraway places that they dreamed of traveling to once the deployment was complete.

One afternoon, I arrived early to begin my 12-hour shift. As I walked into the corner area of the gymnasium-sized operations center, I heard the concluding dialog between some people I worked with. The long and the short of it was that someone was complaining about having to always correct my sloppy work. I was angry when I heard the comment, but I couldn't say that person was wrong. I stewed over those comments for my entire 12-hour shift. I was now living in the moment of dealing with a 3BTO dilemma, and I felt like I'd been kicked by a billy goat.

Identify the Appropriate Standards to Set You Back on Path

If you're ever faced with the 3BTO dilemma, you have to get back to the basics fast. You need to take a look around and figure out what the standards are. If all the things around you have gone to crap, then you need to ask a customer or peer what they think the standard should be.

It will also take research through reports and briefs to get an idea of what the higher levels of leadership are likely looking for in products and service offerings. If you are in an organization that has been making things up as they go along, expect to have challenges. In this case, make a list of three to five questions, then find the smartest person on the subject. Have a 15 minute conversation with that person and try your best to stick to the critical things you need to know. You don't need to flatter them with hollow platitudes, but you do need to explain why you've requested to chat with them. Truth and simplicity trumps everything else; let them know that you view them as the subject matter expert. Oftentimes, in compartmentally-designed organizations, you will have to speak with several people. Make each visit one-on-one to increase your chances for a candid and productive conversation.

Set Your Aspirations Higher Than Average

Your search may take a few days, but if you're diligent, you will be able to establish a baseline for what average looks like. This will be the beginning, the absolute bottom of where you want to be, but it's a great starting point. You can now move forward with the ingredients of what should be in the secret sauce of the growth you seek.

At this point, you need to jot down a few goals for improvement. They should be simple, attainable, and something you can measure. You can (and should) be aspirational, but make sure your goals can yield something that gets you closer on the path to get on the superhighway that leads to your success. Commit to doing things right, with attention to detail, and shake off any negativity you may harbor.

Set Your Boundaries/Limits to Stay on the Path of Greatness

Once you feel decent about the information you have gathered and have the short list of goals you must prioritize, it's critical that you determine where your weight of effort should go first. Interestingly, it may not be your number one goal. It may likely involve changing the way you approach problems or collaborate with people on your team.

During my experience, I initiated my departure from the 3BTO trap by respecting the reason why I was deployed in the first place. I sat on my bunk one morning and made a list of why the work I was doing was important and how it all fit into the larger mission. Things began to "click" after I made my list. I felt a renewed sense of purpose because I embraced the fact that my work was way more important than I initially thought. Sure, I still had times when things didn't go as planned, but I personally saw an improvement. I also no longer thought about how many days I had until I returned home. After a few weeks, I mustered up the courage to ask the team if I was producing better products. The answer was, "Well, you're not hitting home runs, but you're sure hitting some decent balls and getting us closer to where we need to be." Upon hearing that comment, I silently promised myself that I would never visit 3BTO territory again.

CHAPTER #2

Take the First Steps for Growth

"A journey of a thousand miles begins with a single step."
- Lao Tzu

G etting started on a journey of growth can be daunting to many people. The unknown looms ahead, while at least knowing what the current, familiar situation harbors may provide a sense of comfort. You may be reluctant to put forth any forward progress because it seems that the effort will be fruitless. Your first step could be a simple promise to yourself to do better. Although the initial steps might seem awkward, many people around you probably won't notice because they are so engrossed in their own challenges. The key is to get started.

Start with the Performance Plan

As you know, performance plans usually outline the expectations that the company has for employees; it's what we're all measured against. Of course, the types and formats of performance plans can be sliced and diced in many different ways based on skill sets, level of responsibility, and positional authority. The idea is to inform the members of the organization what they need to do in order to be good at their jobs. In most cases, meeting standards puts you right at the 50% category, and since we've already talked about the 3BTO trap, I have a feeling that you want to blaze a different path as an impact player.

Know Performance Plan Standards and the Evaluation Cycle

Years ago, I sat in an office trying to diffuse a situation between a supervisor and a subordinate employee. The problem was about performance on the job, and we were getting nowhere fast. Both parties were nearing their wits' end, and finger pointing was now in full effect. I was still a junior officer and had a bit of trouble understanding why these two otherwise good people were having so many issues. Each of them had over fifteen years of experience, and they seemed okay. After several more minutes of listening to them, I asked to see the performance plan and personal description of duties for the subordinate employee. My request was met with a questioning look from both. In all this time, neither of them had thought about searching the source documents to look at the duties and responsibilities of the employee.

The story above is a good example of why it's critical that we should understand the standards to which we are expected to maintain. In the military, it's relatively straightforward, but there are also some nuances that can catch someone flat footed. One thing that is consistent across all careers is that written standards are available, and you should be very familiar with them. The standards are crucial to attaining the first level of understanding in your position.

A close second is knowing the key dates for the evaluation cycle. Many of us have felt that sinking feeling when we realize that the evaluation date is right around the corner. We rush to gather all the big things we accomplished throughout the evaluation cycle, yet we still feel like it might not be enough meat for the two pages we need to provide as inputs. So, please spare the agony that your future self will have to endure months from now; track the key dates of the performance cycle.

Seek Feedback About What Level of Performance Exceeds Standards

Receiving feedback about what it takes to exceed standards in the organization is like finding a fifty dollar bill on the sidewalk. You feel empathy for the person that never gets it, but you are excited that you received the "gift" just because you were attentive to your surroundings. Getting feedback also means that you have shown your leadership that you're willing to have a conversation about what it takes to be a great contributor to the team.

Feedback can come in many forms. Some leaders prefer to deliver their tips about exceeding standards as a lunch-and-learn event for members of the workforce. Other leaders may prefer to have one-on-one sessions whereby they can deliver a customized session that is targeted to the needs of the individual employee. In all cases, you should be a willing participant in these sessions. Sometimes, you will seemingly walk out of an event without any good takeaways. Regardless, jot down notes of the key points; you may need to refer to them at a later time.

Incorporate Best Practices for Stakeholder Service and Support

Even though the idea of best practices is a proven method for improvement, we sometimes omit them from building a successful performance plan. In some cases, we are so far removed from working directly with a customer or client that we feel like it makes little sense to incorporate. In reality, we should always figure out how the work we do ties into addressing stakeholder requirements. As I mentioned earlier in the book, understanding how the work you do fits into the overall strategy will give you a sense of purpose that can fuel you in your quest for better performance.

As you know, there are entire bodies of work dedicated to helping us identify and incorporate best practices in the work we do each day. It's no small wonder that companies spend a great deal of money hiring outside consultants to help them as they move along the stakeholder service and support continuum. Therefore, it's imperative that you make the effort to find one or two best practices to speak with your evaluator about. Be clear that you would like these to be side items marked as professional development interest areas.

Become an Indispensable Member in the Organization

Whenever I think of people who are indispensable members of an organization, I often think of the unsung heroes. I think of people huddled over their places of work figuring out solutions to problems late into the night. I think of the devoted first responders, teachers, and military service members. I also think of sports team equipment managers. Of all the sports personalities, these are probably the most underrated. It's not debatable that they provide a very essential contribution to the team, but how many of them are on the float during the big parades when the team wins a championship?

Of course, your quest to become an indispensable member in the organization likely won't involve providing sports equipment for a sports team, but you should also understand that indispensable might also mean you won't be famous and highly celebrated in circles outside your organization. You will find that instead, you will be pleased with all that you have accomplished and the appreciation and thanks that you receive from the team you work with.

Set Initial, Short-Term Goals for Your Professional Career

Whenever I started my job at a new duty location, I began my first week with setting my initial, short term goals. Creating the first draft of the goals was always done on a whiteboard where I could step away, tweak the goals after a few days, then finalize them. Since they were short term goals, I always added a "no later than" date for completion. As I began to hone my leadership skills, I always included a goal that I couldn't do alone. It was based on collaboration that needed to occur among the team I was a part of. It challenged me to figure out a way to accomplish a goal that required the buy-in from multiple peers from across other sections or organizations.

Whenever you set a goal in your professional career, you should make sure it fits into the position you currently fill.

Additionally, your goals should be consistent with the career progression of your chosen career path. Of course, the message is different if you plan to pivot from your current profession. For people who intend to move forward in their current career track, you should have a working list of goals. For those of you who are well seasoned, you should dust off those goals you crafted, check off the ones you completed, and get to working on more short-term goals. Try to push yourself by including one to two goals that you will need to collaborate with others to accomplish. Sometimes, the short term goals might take a bit longer than you would like; goals like this offer you an opportunity to reflect on why you didn't complete them. You should appreciate the moments of not getting to your desired end state much in the same way as you treasure the goals you set and knock out of the ballpark.

Understand the Vision and Mission of the Organization

Although it might seem a little basic for me to include, I think it's very important to understand the vision and mission of the organization in which you belong. Sometimes, reading through the vision and mission years after your employee orientation might spark a thought or allow you to finally understand a linkage that you thought was not related. Companies usually devote quite a bit of resources to creating their vision and mission statements. Occasionally, both the vision and mission are created so well that they resonate with a broader audience outside the company and transcend across the market.

Your understanding of both will help you figure out the company culture and even the way they plan to take on future challenges. The important thing to remember is that the vision and mission of a company can change over time. You should be prepared for subtle changes as the company progresses with the evolution of the industry, human resources standards, and the key values of society. That's why it's important to occasionally review both statements.

Focus on 3 + 3 Ideas That Support the Vision & Mission

Once you know the mission and vision, you should begin to think about what goals or initiatives you currently have in place or can develop that align directly with the vision and mission. It goes without saying (but I'm writing it) that your efforts *should* be aligned with the vision and mission. This consistent approach to tasks, ideas, and goals is such a big help; it's almost like having over half the questions of an exam written on the board right in front of you.

I say 3+3 because I believe taking on challenges in chunks of three makes sense, especially when you have big ideas. This also makes it easy for others to process and internalize your concepts. As a rule, have two versions memorized that describe your 3+3 ideas. The first version is the Cliffs Notes, and the second version covers a page with bullet points that we call a talking paper or bullet background paper in the military.

Get the Organization to Invest in Your Professional Development

Some time ago, I received a mass email from the career field office that managed all the logistics officers in the Air Force. The email talked about a one week executive training program on the campus of the University of North Carolina at Chapel Hill. Although I was initially hesitant to apply, I figured giving it a shot wouldn't hurt. Like most professional development opportunities, it was a competitively selected program. I had to complete an application that would be racked and stacked among my peers. The application also called for a variety of recommendation letters, transcripts, and evaluation reports.

A few months later, I found out I was selected for the program. This was one of those pivotal moments because I knew I was really onto something good. The leaders in my career field noticed the positive things I was doing; all my hard work was finally beginning to pay off. This course motivated me to really get focused on becoming a better leader. The program turned out to be one of the best I have ever attended. The lessons I learned over that week with logisticians from the commercial industry were outstanding. As a result, I was able to interact with our industry partners and take home some valuable problem-solving tools and techniques.

Think Like the Business Owner

As you think about the type of skilled workforce needed in today's environment, you should think about this from the perspective of the business owner or company's chief executive officer. Of course, there are the human resource management mandates to follow federal and state laws with no exceptions. There are also widely accepted corporate social responsibilities. Members of the workforce often request and will use the presence (or lack thereof) of these programs to help them determine if they want to remain on the job. Then, in unionized industries, the representatives negotiate with the company leadership to ensure employees receive certain things that make their way into employee compensation packages and the employee handbooks as well.

The company leaders have a lot to think about in the realm of human resource management compliance alone. Once we add the human capital needs of an organization, it becomes quite apparent that there must be a balance between human resources and human capital management. In most cases, both fall under the umbrella of HR, but it's important to keep the distinction in mind because they do go hand in glove, and many times, it's hard for non-HR-trained people to see any difference. I have been in meetings where senior leaders debate for hours about initiatives, intent, and what part of the budget should be allocated.

Ask the Key Question: Why Would Someone Want to Invest in My Growth?

As you work on your plan for professional development, you must ask the one crucial question: Why should the organization invest in me? If your answer starts and ends with "Because I'm a great person," you will need to do some serious reflection. I have no doubt that you are a great person because you're reading this book, but unfortunately, that answer won't get you too far.

The first thing you need to do is pull out a blank sheet of legal paper or preferred software to build your matrix. On the top, write something related to what you're doing, but make it humorous. This is so you will smile every time you read it. You will need to be in a cheerful mood when you do this exercise. Next, set up your columns with headings: top five opportunities that interest me, directly related to my job (yes or no), event dates, criteria and requirements, cost, my top five accomplishments with the company, and finally, bring over your short term goals to make sure the potential opportunity aligns with your previously established goals. Don't worry, if it doesn't perfectly align, maybe it's just time to modify one or more of your goals.

After all this work comes the "fun" part. Whittle your list of opportunities to two, then make sure those are aligned with your current role. Next, start producing a document that talks through the details of the upcoming opportunity, highlights your accomplishments, and gives the top three reasons why you're the ideal candidate for this opportunity. You will eventually need to send this to your boss. We'll talk about those next steps later in the book.

Invest in Yourself

There's no substitute for investing resources in yourself to become better at something. We sometimes have a standoffish feeling about committing our personal resources for training or professional growth activities. Raise your hand if you've ever heard someone, or even said to yourself, "If the company wanted me to know this X, they should have sent me to training for my X certification (fill in the blanks)." While in some cases this is spot on, in many cases, you're limiting your personal and professional growth. That particular certification or skill set is usually highly transferable; you can easily use it in other jobs or positions for growth inside and outside the company.

In all cases, you should conduct thorough research to ensure the investment you make will be worthwhile. Sometimes, you will pay a few thousand dollars for training, so you need to do a quick analysis to determine your return on investment. If it's training the company values, they might reimburse you for the training, so be sure to negotiate this before you pay for the training out of pocket.

In other cases, the training may not cost any money but will require a significant time commitment. Be wary of falling into the trap of thinking that you're so busy that you can't do the training at this time. I've seen this happen so many times with people in the military. After serving many years, they create a great deal of stress trying to catch up so they can continue moving up in ranks. They spend so much time focused on the mission that they neglect self care and personal enrichment. Take control of your destiny and invest in yourself.

CHAPTER #3

The 6 Things You Need to Know

"Knowledge is power."

- Sir Francis Bacon

The tension in the room was high on that day in March 2003 as we all gathered in the operations center to get the latest news about what was going on. It had been hours since the communications blackout, and everyone was beginning to speculate about what was going on in the world. Over the course of several months, we had seen the steady build up of forces in the region, but we weren't really sure if it would lead to anything significant. I was temporarily lost in my thoughts about our next strategic move.

Just then, the aide-de-camp yelled, "Room, 'tench huuut'!" We all stood rigidly at attention as the General strode into the room and shouted, "At ease." As we relaxed our stance, he quickly got down to the brass tacks of what was going on. The General explained the current situation and talked about what we needed to do to ensure success throughout the campaign. Many people had smiles of assurance on their faces, and most of us nodded our heads in unison to convey our acknowledgement of the key points he provided in the update. In about five minutes, he gave us all the information we needed to know for us to do the very best we could to support our troops as they made the push across the border and into harm's way.

Underpin Your Growth with Foundational Attributes

A sturdy foundation of knowledge means the difference between success and failure. In an optimal situation, we have the luxury of an adequate period of time to learn and experience what we need in order to be successful. In military circles, an "adequate" time frame depends on the urgency of the situation and the desired effect. Although in low threat, permissive environments you can afford to bank on the slow progression of challenges that comes with a gradual increase in duties and responsibilities. There's really something to be appreciated in having the time to get settled into a new position or job. On the other hand, there are times when you step into a high operational tempo organization where you're putting out dumpster fires like some kind of video game.

Ideally, you will never have to deal with the high stress of a fast-paced job where you don't have the time to develop foundational attributes for your growth, but the reality is that either you're living in this moment, you have lived this life (and will again), or this life will soon be your reality. Therefore, it makes sense for you to take the steps to learn how to reduce the time and pain you experience during the ascent up the steep learning curve.

A Sturdy Foundation Facilitates Explosive Acceleration

A sturdy foundation is essential for quickly moving forward; it acts as your springboard. Forward movement is awfully difficult unless there's something to use as a proper source of friction. Without a springboard or starting block, you will expend tons of energy in the beginning but will make very little progress compared to your peers.

Over the course of my career, I have worked hard on developing the foundational tools for my accelerated growth strategy. I started out at my first duty assignment with little guidance or direction from the commander or my immediate supervisor on what it takes to be great. The one thing my supervisor did tell me was that I should take a writing course to become a better writer; he really did me a solid on that one. Another thing I picked up from the first Senior Non-Commissioned Officer I worked with was that I needed to create a daily routine. While he didn't specifically say I should build good habits, his talk with me was the catalyst that prompted me to work on things that would lead me to greater growth and positive change. So, it's no small wonder that the first two areas I focused on as a military officer and continue to work hard on today are using clear and concise communications and building powerful habits.

I've met some brilliant people who are subject matter experts in their chosen career fields. I mean, these people have many professional degrees and prestigious awards for the work they do. The only problem is that they would be hard pressed and stressed out if they had to provide a one page summary. For one, they would have a hard time distilling the information into one page; they need to include every bit of information. Secondly, they would have so much jargon in the document that you would need to have a decoder ring handy to figure out what all the alphabet soup was all about.

Sure, there's a time and place for that level of detail, especially if you're talking about flying or an aircraft maintenance instruction. However, if a person cannot communicate clearly and concisely, there's a strong likelihood that their journey and promotion to the higher levels will be harder. These are the people that are well paid but pigeonholed. They may even have official translators that are part of their teams. If you've seen this happen, then you know what I mean.

The other attribute is building *good* powerful habits. I emphasize **good** because we live in the world of the latest faze and craze taking over social media and the lives of many people by storm. Literally, it's like a storm that enters the market and stays for a while until most people know about it. Remember, just because a powerful habit is trending upward on social media or has garnered the latest cult-like following, that doesn't mean it's a quality habit that will actually help *you* succeed.

Trust me, after a short time, the copycats arrive at the market to capitalize on the fad and do it better than the originator. Then, one day, everything seemingly disappears as it is replaced by another "great" something. Lots of people call that good marketing, but in terms of staying power, I know it creates a bullwhip effect on many people. These everyday folks are thrown all about as the disrupter enters the market like a hail storm on a hot July day and later departs after a finale that ends with someone left picking up the pieces in bewilderment. The powerful habit you thought would change you forever ends up hidden away in the darkest corner of the closet as a painful reminder of your unwarranted enthusiasm.

So, here are the first two things you need to know:

- Communicate Clearly
- Build a Powerful Routine

Develop a Strong Center of Gravity

If you've ever watched any of the great football running backs, you'll notice that they keep their centers of gravity in check. Many of these athletes are shorter than most football players, hence, they have a lower center of gravity. It seems like they defy the laws of physics as people hit them with the force of a jackhammer, yet they bounce off and keep moving as if they were in a children's bouncy castle. They also train to move quickly, as speed and agility are in top order when faced with obstacles that could certainly change the forward progress to a zero gain or even worse a loss of time and any positive gains made before.

Although you won't be running on a football field trying to get across the goal line, you will have to be ready with the techniques to overcome the things that may stand in your path for success. When it comes to pushing yourself to the next level, the need for a strong center of gravity applies in terms of planning and demonstrating your value to others. Having these core attributes will keep you moving on task when facing the constraints of time or mission limitations.

A Strong Center of Gravity Allows You to Lean Into Challenges

We will all experience challenges throughout our lives. Some people may seemingly get a worse deal than others, but it also depends on the perspective from the foxhole you sit in. Having a deliberate plan about what you want to do, when you want to do it, and how it will be done is a great start.

Deliberate planning has been a mainstay in the military and business for decades. One of the major differences that evolved over the past twenty years is the incorporation of agile practices. Agile helps us lean into adversity because we learn from every iteration. We tweak things based on feedback and can look at challenges through the lens differently. Those challenges become valuable as we unearth some positive changes throughout the process of developing a solution.

Just as deliberate planning provides the framework for all that we do, our sense of value gives us the mental stability we need to drive forward. Your personal value is uniquely yours. There's no one else like you, and there won't be anyone that can ever make the same impression on an organization. Nowadays, the common expression is that you need to own it. You must realize your value early, then seek the right opportunities to show the value you bring to the organization. Maybe your contribution of value is small at first, but over time, things will snowball. It takes a willingness to take on some calculated challenges. If you learn the lessons in this book, you will be better suited to take on challenges with confidence and excitement as you hone your skills in the high operational tempo environment.

Chapters 6 and 7 provide a greater, detailed explanation of these two areas that make up our framework for success.

- Create a Deliberate Plan
- Demonstrate Your Value

Accelerate Your Pace with Unflappable Confidence

Have you ever watched a basketball game that was one sided before the half? One team was getting clobbered, while the other team was on easy street and could be seen along the sidelines already giving each other high fives. The losing team seemed to be trying hard but weren't having the best of luck. Watching the game may seem like a waste of time.

As the ball sails through the air with the tip off after the half, you see that the losing team is working hard to get points on the board. In spite of being down by twenty points, they begin to make up the points deficit. They do it first by changing their outlook. You are struck by the way the team is playing with better posture, and even the folks on the sidelines have moved up to the edge of their seats. As the final seconds of the game begin to wind down, they are now within one point of winning the game. You watch with excitement as the losing team passes the ball to their star player, who takes a shot from the three-point line. As the game clock is down to tenths of a second, the shot goes in the air and falls right between the nets. It's not called a buzzer beater for nothing.

Just like we have seen many times in sports, we must not be deterred when starting a bit behind our colleagues. Maybe they were already on the job when you arrived, or maybe you had a minor setback for a few weeks. Nevertheless, you have to get back into the game and produce. You must clearly know your purpose. Sometimes, we have the luxury of the half to gather our thoughts, reflect on what we can do better, then go back out there and claw our way to contention. In many cases, we don't have the good fortune of time to reset, so we have to rely on our resilience. Instead of wallowing in what already is, we have to move bravely ahead in the current space where we are and exist in the now.

Moving with a Sense of Purpose

When I arrived at Lackland Air Force Base in San Antonio, Texas for Air Force officer field training, I was a hot mess. I stepped off the bus to the yelling of military training instructors as I was directed to stand on the painted footprints at the bus depot. It almost felt like an out of body experience as I grabbed my bags and hustled away to find the open bay barracks that would be my home for the next four weeks. My body was soaked with so much sweat that one of the cadet training officers made me stop and take a few swigs of water from the canteen, as I must have looked like I was close to having a heat stroke. Throughout that first day, all I seemed to hear being shouted by the cadet training officers and training instructors was the phrase, "Move with a sense of purpose!" I still smile when thinking about that tough day and never shall forget it.

Moving with the right sense of purpose is essential for what you're going to do. If you want to have a transformational experience, then you have to move with purpose. We can all probably think of what wasted effort looks like. We definitely don't want to shortchange ourselves or attempt to trick ourselves into believing that there's no work involved in making a change. You will find that you have to do some work to get proficient at anything. If you want to quickly move forward and move up the ranks, you must build your personal strategy with the tools and techniques offered in this book.

The final two techniques you need to master are the traits and practices of a purposeful leader, and you must be a willing practitioner of mindful evaluation and reflection. These are the two "bring it on home" attributes because they involve the most introspective time. When you read these two chapters, you need to really internalize what you learn by pulling out a journal and reflecting on all that you have learned along the way.

- Be a Purposeful Leader
- Evaluate and Reflect

I hope you're just as excited as I am for you to get started on your journey to overcoming the challenges of the tumultuous ten. Let's swiftly move to the mission objective with **boldness, brilliance,** and **benevolence!**

CHAPTER #4

Communicate Clearly

"Examine what is said, not who is speaking."
                                    - African Proverb

I sat in the back of the conference room with my notebook and pen in hand, trying my best to capture every word the General was speaking. I wasn't sure about all the details he was referring to, but I scribbled anyway. It was part of the duties I fulfilled while working as a junior officer at the Pentagon. Over the months, I had gained the confidence of my boss and was allowed to attend some meetings as a third (or fourth) set of ears.

At the conclusion of the meeting, we hurried back to our office to decipher the notes and talk about the products we were ordered to create. I treated the follow-up meeting like a grown up version of the game telephone. It always surprised me whenever there was a disconnect between two or more of us regarding what the General said in the meeting. Sometimes, we all shook our heads in frustration, but most times, I was appointed to make the trip to the General's office to speak with the Executive Officer, who also attended many of the meetings. I would seek clarification from him, since he was assigned with me years prior at my first duty assignment on Guam. Occasionally, he would even walk into the General's office to quickly seek clarification. I would hover, hidden just outside the door, listening intently to the General's reply. Having that relationship with the Exec was a tremendous help to my survival as a staff officer at the Pentagon. It's also a good reason why you always want to ensure you understand the message.

Understand the Task You're Asked to Do

When I first entered the Air Force many years ago, I was a greenhorn. Sometimes, I was the butt of playful jokes between young butter bars and the NCOs, which didn't bother me. I knew that the butter bars I wore screamed to all that I was the new guy and I didn't know crap. Since I was stationed on the small island of Guam, the whole group of us second lieutenants hung out with each other after work and on the weekends.

The conversation was usually either about work or sports. I preferred to talk about work since I was fascinated with the way different squadrons and groups conducted their operations. I particularly liked to hear the stories about internal and external communication, how they published guidance, and how they conducted staff meetings. I tried not to say too much to break up the stories because I was in constant receive mode. I was trying to soak up all the tools of the trade so that I could devise my personal list of best practices based on either someone bragging or complaining about what they had gone through at work.

Many times, the difference between joy and pain was whether or not they had accurately received and acted on the task their boss had communicated to them. Since email at far-flung places like Guam was still in its infancy, most taskers were either captured during meetings, sent out by the secretaries on official task lists, or were "drive-by" taskers. Those drive-by taskers were the worst since they usually happened at the end of the day when a supervisor or senior leader decided it was time to come out to the work areas. When you saw them in your area, you had better get a notebook because things were going to come at you fast like the rounds coming out of a 50 mm Gatling gun.

I learned early on that if you took down a task and the leaders saw you, they wouldn't ask for it early to remind you. Portable, electronic calendars were not around, so there was nothing to remind you when it was due. Also, writing a tasker down without asking for any clarification was acknowledging that you understood what was being requested and you would have it done just as prescribed. Some of the tougher leaders also didn't give you much recourse if you underestimated how long it would take for you to complete the request. The product was due on the date and time when they said it needed to be done. For the first few months, I stumbled to get things done correctly. It seemed like nothing could go my way. After a few months of feeling the pain, I reached out to my lieutenant friends.

My buddies quickly informed me that I needed to leverage the most powerful resource I had at hand, the Senior Non-Commissioned Officer (SNCO). They walked me through a couple of scenarios where I asked for help. The next time I was faced with the visit of leadership, I literally ran and got a hold of a SNCO. During the interactions, something amazing happened. Whenever there was something that wasn't fully understood, the SNCO requested that the information be restated or the SCNO began his reply with, "So what you're asking is this, right?" The information became a lot clearer to me, and once I saw these kinds of interactions a few times, that one technique began to help me get out of hot water and stay out.

Slow Down the Train

All of us routinely communicate with nonverbal cues. We might change our posture, gaze, overall body position, or facial expression when speaking with someone. The nod that we initiate when listening to someone make a request, ask us a question, or give us a task to perform is one of the biggest nonverbals. Nodding is the easiest thing to do to show that you read someone loud and clear.

For the purpose of accelerating your growth, try to avoid nodding when someone is asking you to do something. It's incredibly difficult to do. You will likely find yourself shifting to doing something like clicking a pen or rocking side to side in their presence if you are not on a video call. The reason why it's so hard is that we want to affirm that we understand what they are saying: "Read you loud and clear." The trouble is that sometimes we don't have a clear understanding of what we're being asked to do.

Oftentimes, the requestor leaves thinking that they have gotten their point across and will expect to receive the "thing" from you just as they had requested it. We leave the meeting feeling like we understand, too. That is until we have a few more minutes to process all the data that we heard and realize, "Oh gosh, there are gaps in the information." We are left with little choice but to send an email requesting clarification on the whole task, which in turn makes the requestor upset because they have to pause and reflect on what they actually told you. Then, we enter the twilight zone, because it starts feeling like both parties must have dreamed up the whole meeting.

Of course, we can't really move forward with our plans until we get a clarification email because we would hate to get started on the "thing" only to find out that it wasn't supposed to be done that way. So, what are we going to do, since it's due in two days? Well, we figure we can at least map out what we do know to prevent us wasting too much time. Then, we come up with a few things we can start doing to get us a bit closer to producing the product as well.

Okay, let's circle back to the beginning of this scenario. The meeting was going on, and you were listening intently, except this time, you weren't nodding along. If no other colleagues are there, you won't have anyone to corroborate what was said. You desperately need to get the barrage of information to stop momentarily so you can get your bearings.

Although you can't yell, "Please stop for a minute," you can jump in there and ask a question regarding something that was said earlier in the conversation. If you don't slow down the train, you run the risk of losing it all and spending precious time spinning your wheels for hours, if not days. So, you manage to get the pause you need, and afterwards, you do a very quick review to make sure you understand what they have said to this point in the conversation. At the very least, you can request approval for you to send them a clarification email to make sure you heard the right things. Giving them a warning that a clarification email is coming is a lot better than letting it stew for a while, then having to send an email anyway.

The Last Minute Question

We have all attended meetings that felt so long that, by the time it was close to the end, we felt like we'd been out all day at an amusement park in August with no water to drink. Then, just as we were about to celebrate the meeting being done, someone pops up their hand and says, "I have a question. Can you please clarify X, Y, and Z?" In your mind, you're thinking about taking that person off your Christmas card list.

When this happens, you just have to take a deep breath, right? You know how it feels when a question is raised at the tail end of a meeting. Please make it a practice not to do this yourself. I know you're thinking that this is basic office etiquette, but you have to be mindful of this as you progress up the hierarchy in the company.

Of course, it does make sense when you know everybody is waiting for someone else to ask the question. If you take one for the team, people will remember you for your bravery. In cases like that, you and your colleagues need to rotate who takes it for the team. If you're always the one asking the question, then your co-workers are setting you up. Don't be the hero each and every time; someone else needs an opportunity, too.

Avoid the Rumor Mill

Communications sources within the organization are varied and can be based on rumor, not on fact. Avoid feeding anything into the gossip ecosystem. It's common sense, right? However, there are always things that start out as good deeds or heads up which might be based on facts that aren't yet releasable to the public or perhaps never will be released if you work for a private company. I'm not talking about things that are legally wrong. What I'm targeting here are those things that are usually best handled by the HR department. Stay in your lane on these types of communications.

Take a Formal Class

Earlier in the book, I talked about the supervisor at my first duty location who told me to take a writing course. Initially, I was a little taken aback because I'd just graduated college only a few months prior. What he should have said was, "Learn how to write your own performance reports and understand what it takes to accurately capture all the good things you do in your position. Of course, I eventually took the writing course at another duty location. It was very helpful, and moving forward, I usually provided all my supervisors with a ready-to-go version of emails to higher headquarters, my performance report, end of tour decoration, letters of recommendation, and any other correspondence they needed from either me or the organization I was in charge of. I made it easy for them, and as a result, they greatly appreciated all the work I put into saving them time.

There are many people who complain how they weren't given a fair shake on their performance report. It turns out these people provided little to contribute to the writing of their report. If your place of work doesn't offer any type of training, head over to the local junior college to take a night class on whatever writing you do the most on the job and what is used in your evaluation. It will pay for itself quickly, and you will feel a lot better knowing that you have accomplished yet another goal.

Delivering Accurate Reports

During one of my deployments, I had to travel over to an Army tactical operations center (TOC) once a week. As soon as you walked into the TOC, there was a poster with the following message from the battle captain:

- The first report is always wrong
- Who else needs to know
- It takes longer than it takes
- What else can be done
- There's always one more thing you can do

I found each bullet point to be straightforward and highly relatable to life in a combat environment. Over the years, I developed a mental checklist based on these points. I incorporated them into my life once I returned from that particular deployment. They were especially useful when I was awakened in the middle of the night by a phone call from the command post or operations center in the wake of an unfortunate incident or an emergency operations update. Although you're not facing the dangers of combat or other operations, you can use these points to assist in the way you gather, interpret, and act on information.

Dealing with Information Overload

Years ago, we thought we had it bad enough with the 50 or 60 emails we might get in a single day. Then, the email bugs came along and totally screwed up our schedules as we seemed to all get the bug at the same time, bringing things to a snail's pace. We spent so much time on building charts and other briefing products that were changed so many times that some had hundreds of editing hours before the final 30 minute brief was presented to senior leadership in the military.

In this day and age, we are constantly bombarded with information in our everyday lives. Today, our email inboxes are usually full within minutes of us cleaning them out. We use digital assistants to keep us organized and the emails prioritized, but right now, they require a human touch to ensure important information doesn't inadvertently fall through the cracks.

As you routinely face the onslaught of information, you must conduct a swift analysis to find crucial ties and junction points that can support what task you are trying to complete. Save yourself some pain. Enlist the aid of data-mining tools to help you sort, consolidate, and prepare, because the key is to filter through information quickly. I used the 5 Ws (Who, What, When, Where, Why) as a starting point.

> Don't become a slave to the email inbox. It will likely never be empty.

Leverage the weekly staff meeting as a place to synchronize with others regarding what's going on. If your organization conducts daily scrum meetings, then you're already ahead of others. If you don't do a daily meeting when you're working on a major deliverable, consider implementing this practice. Keep the timing tight and make it productive. The daily meeting is not when you want to be talking about the concert you attended the night before. Additionally, you need to know what's important to your boss and higher levels of company leadership. In the next section, we'll talk about the importance of timing.

Timing

When we step through the mechanics of a great communications plan at the individual level, we can't ignore the effect of timing, since our primary purpose is showing you how to decrease the time in which you need to get up to speed and make a positive impact.` Once you get information on your task, you have to put it against a timeline to figure out the priority and estimated completion date. Write this down first, because it will serve as a good resource to look back on to track your productivity. Once you have the estimate, determine if you need to add any days for the back and forth between you and your boss. Finally, add the amount of time it will take to staff the product through all the areas of the organization. With the electronic processes most organizations have in place, coordination and approval should be easier than it once was.

If you're working on a collaborative project, try to be the project lead. Set up your timeline to incorporate the extra few days it may take to form a cross functional team and get it to a point of smooth operations. Remember, the things you've already learned about rocky first meetings and short term friction among new teammates is real. Keep the team focused with a combination of sprints to get things done and very active collaboration with an emphasis on your schedule during your engagements, not to the point of obsession, but to ensure you move with a sense of purpose like we talked about earlier in the book.

Use Collaborative Tools and Incorporate Feedback

Information sharing is a powerful tool. Earlier, we talked about making sure you capture the correct information during engagements, and we talked about information overload. Great news! Since the COVID-19 pandemic, most people have embraced and use online collaboration tools. This places you at a huge advantage, because not only can you collaborate with the people that you work with, but there's also an opportunity to collaborate with other people that belong to your community of interest. Normally, these communities of interest reside within professional organizations and certifying bodies that have an international presence. If you discuss any work-related topics, make sure it doesn't violate any company policies, and don't share briefs or working papers to ensure you're not giving away any information that may be detrimental to your company in the marketplace.

I will stress the importance of feedback and self-reflection throughout this book. As you know, it can be formal or informal depending on the nature of the product or task you're working to complete. I think it's best to get feedback while you're still working on the project to facilitate learning and improvement. Also, get a variety of feedback from various levels in your organization. It's very important that you seek feedback from your peers and upper supervision. You're working to achieve rapid acceleration and growth, and the only way to do that is to get vector checks along the way.

Recovering from Miscues

Many years ago, I was working on an event for over 300 people. Although I was only one cog in the wheel, I had an important role in setting up the opening ceremony for a well-respected retired General Officer. On the night of the event, several members of our committee dressed up in our camouflage uniforms to make a dramatic entry. We hopped into a big combat assault vehicle and began to drive down the flightline.

At the indicated rally point, the General joined us in the vehicle. With radio in hand, I called for the other team several times for them to get in place, as they were supposed to stage a simulated ambush. To my dismay, all I heard was crickets, nothing, nada on the radio. I waited for about 30 seconds while the General sat patiently in the vehicle. I called the final time, and there wasn't an answer. Decision time and gut check. So, I nodded to the General, received his thumbs up, then gave the go, go, go order to the driver. We entered the area with great fanfare, the general received a standing ovation for his part, and I quickly disappeared in the backdrop. I later learned that the other team was on a different channel, therefore they heard nothing. It was a miscue that I will always remember because the mistake was so simple. The lesson learned: make sure both groups know what radio channel you're going to be on – both literally and figuratively.

Rule #1: Admit the Mistake

The first rule when you have a communications miscue is to admit if you were the one that screwed up. It's like ripping off the band-aid: painful at first, but an essential part of moving on. As the adage goes, nobody is perfect. Be prepared for the fallout that will come your way, but don't let the thought of your screwup eat away at you for more than a day or two. If it's a big screwup, expect to be disciplined, even though it wasn't intentional. You have to understand that this will be a setback, but don't let it deter you from moving forward with the other aspects of your accelerated growth plan.

Have a plan in place before your boss asks if you have a remedy. If there's an internal checklist, be sure to start going through it line by line; be thorough and complete with any information you provide. Also, be realistic in how you're going to fix the problem and how long it's going to take to return to normality. If it's related to another department or impacts them in any way, call your peer in the other area. Explain to them about the fallout that will be coming their way soon. Even a short notice call can help them start running their own recovery efforts. They won't be happy, so don't try to make light of the situation unless they initiate the comedy or irony of the situation. Help them formulate a get-well plan as much as you can from your perspective.

Next, contact any external stakeholders if you're permitted to by your leadership. A sincere phone call or video chat will often go a long way. Explain the situation to them. Be careful with your language and details. If it's a really sensitive issue, have someone from the legal counsel present in the meeting, and maybe someone from one of the other areas in the company if needed. They will also want to speak with a subject matter expert, so have that person or group of people available. Schedule another update call to keep the stakeholders in the loop.

> Although rarely needed, seek the assistance of outside counsel if the company is pressing to take legal action against you.

Prepare for the internal investigation. Keep all the pertinent documents of the event to include meeting minutes of the talk with the stakeholders. Prepare any required documents and keep all emails related to the subject. Although rarely needed, seek the assistance of outside counsel if the company is pressing to take legal action against you. Seek out the help of experts in the company, and don't try to do everything by yourself, because you will likely overlook something.

Solve the Problem

As you work your way through the solution, call in experts as required. As stated before, don't try to fix the problem all by yourself. Avoid the temptation to spare others the extra work because you would rather fix the problem all the way than partially. Once resolved, you don't want to have to revisit, and neither does anyone else. If you need additional resources, contact your supervisor for assistance. If the solution doesn't fit, you can't force it. You may have to think of another way.

Fixing the problem may take you far longer than you anticipated, so make sure you keep the right people updated regarding your progress. If it's big, you may have to set up a small team. If that is the case, make sure all the proper introductions occur and the purpose of the team is clearly understood by all parties. Understand that the ad hoc team probably won't like being there to fix a problem. Find ways to enhance their quality of life if they're putting in extra hours. There won't be a social after the problem is resolved and the team disbands, but see if there is some way to recognize the team for their efforts, even if it's just a letter of appreciation from your supervisor to all the members that pitched in.

Move Forward: Build Red Teaming Into Your Communications Strategy

As you move forward through the recovery and solution phases, evaluate what you did wrong and how it could have been mitigated. Of course, I know you will be doing this in tandem with working through the solution, but don't let the red teaming get in your way of solving the problem as soon as you can. The red team should be carried out with a few members. Expect to feel the sting from the analysis. Also, ask to get a copy of the report if there's an internal review. Along those same lines, set up internal controls to make sure this miscue won't happen again. Expect to get audited a few times by internal review, as the company will use the audit to determine if you have adequate controls in place.

There's a lot of information about communicating. My objective for this chapter was two-fold. I want you to get comfortable knowing that you need to communicate using the best methods available, and I also wanted to remind you that it's going to be "okay" if you occasionally have a communication snafu. Although the recovery may be challenging, it's not impossible to overcome.

Get ready! The next chapter about building a powerful routine puts things into a higher gear as we continue to build a sturdy foundation. The following information found in chapter 5 will be the catalyst for your explosive acceleration. I'm very excited for you to read on, I know you will benefit greatly.

CHAPTER #5

Build a Powerful Routine

"We are what we repeatedly do. Excellence then, is not an act, but a habit. "

- Aristotle

I am fascinated by the routines of long distance runners. On race day, they perform incredible feats of endurance, as they often undergo extreme trials and tribulations during the race, especially if they want to win. You can often see the agony in the face of each runner as they hit the wall, yet something keeps them going past that point. This is when it doesn't matter how good of shape they're in; it's simply going to hurt. Yet there are still more miles to go before crossing the finish line, so maybe their obsession to finish keeps them moving forward one stride at a time.

The elite racers look as if they are gliding along on the course. They have a singular purpose in mind of getting to the finish line ahead of all the rest. Many times, it ends up being a close race, as a handful of runners usually pull away from the pack and begin to vie for position to win. The last half mile must be tough, as the leaders of the pack are all running on fumes. I think the endorphins have served their purpose, so at this point, they are in a euphoric state; the out of body experience is real.

What intrigues me even more is the time and energy all distance runners spend preparing for a race. All the miles they spend training alone. They are out there, hitting the pavement for weeks ahead of the race. They run in both good weather and crappy weather. They run on weekdays and weekends, before or after work. These folks just love to run, and they understand the importance of having a routine to the point where it's probably more of a ritual. So, to all the long distance and ultra runners out there; I'm sending you a double high five and two thumbs up.

In order to be successful, you don't have to be a long distance runner, but you do have to be willing to devote time and energy to building a powerful routine. You must have the discipline to hone your skills through learning and practicing on a daily basis. The pace should make you feel uncomfortable, but you should lean into it hard to see the best results. Unlike the runner, there's no rest for you at the finish line; you must keep moving forward. Building and maintaining your powerful routine is a vocation. We should all strive to be better and do better, so eventually we can help others grow and accelerate, too.

Eliminate Wasteful Habits

When I was a small kid, one of my favorite pastimes was watching cartoons and game shows on weekday mornings. I was too young to go to school, so I stayed at home while my aunt kept me throughout the day. I woke up really early so I could catch those programs. I happily sat there in front of the television and watched cartoons and game shows all morning.

When the summer finally arrived and the weather warmed up, my aunt no longer allowed me to watch television. I had to go play outside. When I protested, she gently told me that I needed to stop watching television so much because I wouldn't be able to do that once I started kindergarten. I was very sad. As I look back on that experience, I think it was the first time someone told me that I needed to change a habit that was robbing me of a better, more memorable day. She was absolutely right.

Start the Big Change Now

Getting started on something, anything is often hard to do, especially if there's a lot at stake. Sometimes, if you don't act, nothing bad will happen; you'll just remain in the same place. Other times, inaction can lead to the negative consequence of losing out on experiencing new and exciting things that can enrich your life and the lives of others that you care about.

You may be hesitant to move as you survey the surrounding area and begin to explore the possibilities of jumpstarting your career. That inner voice of doubt may tell you to wait a little longer, settle into the job more, or remain under the radar. Yet, there's also something inside giving you a little nudge of encouragement. Or, perhaps it's the assuring voice of a friend or colleague telling you to give it a shot.

Even though you may not feel ready, take the first steps. Maybe it won't be a leap, only a shuffle forward, but at least it's movement. That small movement will start the gears of change that begin the process of defeating the constraints of physics. The motion, however slight it may seem, will be the catalyst for the monumental commencement of amazing and fulfilling growth that is life changing.

> "An object at rest remains at rest, and an object in motion remains in motion at a constant speed and in a straight line unless acted on by an unbalanced force."
> - Sir Issac Newton's First Law of Motion (Inertia)

Eliminate Habits that Hold You Back

If you walk down a busy street, there's a strong chance that you will see multiple people engaged in doing or not doing "stuff." For example, you will likely see a multitude of people looking at their phone. Some are viewing the world through the phone instead of seeing it outside of the pixelated screen with their own eyes. We've all been to those events where a person is so engrossed in recording a concert or event on their phone that they aren't truly living in the moment. This is similar to looking through the lens of a bad habit. It distorts reality in a way that prevents you from seeing the true wonders of what your life *could* be like. Perhaps the habit may involve an unhealthy routine like consuming a meal or snack that the physician has warned may lead to health consequences.

You don't know what a person's unproductive habit is. Although we shouldn't be overly judgemental in our views of others, we must work to reduce and eventually eliminate the bad habits that can diminish or chip away from the positive gains we've made. If you have a questionable habit, please reevaluate today. If it doesn't add value to your growth plan, begin the process of removal.

Since no one knows you better than you know yourself, you must rely on introspection. Identify one to three current practices you would like to eliminate or modify to a point where they no longer feel like excess cargo slowing you down. Once you have your list, figure out one thing you can do each day to reduce the impact of the bad habit. Then, work hard until you've eliminated it completely; take as long as you need since you're fighting a daily battle. If you slip a little, make a commitment to do better the next day. In many cases, you should think of this process as being a wonderful gift of thoughtfulness from your current self to your future self.

Strengthen Your Positive Habits

Just as you have a few non-productive habits that are perfect candidates to eliminate, there are also some habits that you want to strengthen. Stopping a wasteful habit takes energy to overcome the impact of speed and force of the negative. Nurturing a positive habit takes focus and a level of commitment that requires you to be driven to do better each day. At first glance, it may seem easier to increase the speed of improvement because you're already doing it, but the incremental changes required to get better are sometimes difficult. They are difficult because you have to monitor the little details that come along with trying to get just a bit better each day. Most of us appreciate the concept of small improvements along the way, but how many of us have the patience of staying on the path of change?

Consider strengthening a positive habit as being similar to growing a majestic oak tree from a small acorn. The tree starts from a small seedling, and there are critical junctures along the way that you must implement in order to achieve the objective of growing a big, strongly rooted oak tree. Yet, it takes a while to observe any significant change, especially in that dormant phase where the magic is happening just underneath the surface.

Growing that seedling into a healthy and majestic shade tree takes lots of effort. So will nurturing and strengthening your positive habits. You have to be methodical in your planning and approach by writing down what you plan to improve, then charting the improvements you make along the way. Stepping through the process of strengthening your habits will require you to narrow your routine to the things that matter with a laser-like focus. In the military, we call this process zeroing your scope. I also call this prioritizing your priorities to achieve greater clarity and purpose.

Prioritize Your Priorities

When I was in college, I worked at a variety of places to help with the cost of tuition and living expenses. In relative terms, things were very expensive, even though I attended college eons ago. For a while, I worked second shift at a factory and attended school during the morning and afternoons. It was truly a grind, and I often returned after work to my efficiency apartment past midnight. I was always tired, broke, and spinning my wheels trying to make it through my classes.

This experience was the first time that I had to prioritize everything about my life, and it was very difficult. One day, as

I was nodding off to sleep in my 8:00 a.m. class, the instructor walked over and kindly asked me to leave the class. That ordeal stung a lot; I was teetering on the edge, headed for failure. I stood outside the door for another 15 minutes until the class ended. Afterwards, the instructor and I had a candid 2 minute chat. After that conversation, I knew that I needed to prioritize my priorities if I ever wanted to make it through college, let alone the class. That day, I left the class with clarity about my situation. I had to make a decision as to whether I would remain a college student or pack it all up and head back home to South Carolina. I chose to prioritize my priorities, which meant giving up the job and figuring out another way to make ends meet. I'm very glad I did.

Understand the Connectedness of Your Priorities

As part of the foundational attributes for your rapid growth plan, setting priorities for your powerful routine is like choosing a trail to reach a destination. Also, think of your priorities as being interconnected, concentric rings that can be labeled: self, family, and external (job). Self lies in the center of it all for obvious reasons, since you must make sure you're fully oriented and on task before you can devote your energies on other priorities.

Of course, as good people trying to do the right thing, we typically put the priorities of others before our own. Many times, it may seem unavoidable, especially when it comes to shuffling your life around due to the needs of your family or close friends. And we can't leave out what happens if we have a surge of activity at work that may disrupt the normal rhythm of our life for days, weeks, or months.

In times of relative calm, you should give a shot at writing down your priorities, the priorities of your family, and priorities for improving performance at your company. At first, it may be difficult to determine, but at least create a simple framework on a piece of butcher paper. Get those sticky notes out, then start writing and posting them. Of course, you can do this alone or with the help of a significant other. Once you get the priorities down on paper, you'll visually see the overlaps and perhaps see potential synergies. In addition, you can start thinking about outcomes and desired end states; i.e., the "so what?"

Pivot and Flex

Most times, things change quite often in our lives as we start our growth journey and move forward. Throughout our journey, we learn how to pivot and flex as we react to various challenges in our environment. I think it's a part of the safety mechanism in the reptilian brain that governs this natural ability to survive. Although we don't face the dangers of survival in our personal and professional lives as if a grizzly bear is chasing us down a hillside, we still have legitimate reasons for pivoting and flexing based on our environment.

As you're actively working through accomplishing your career priorities, expect to have setbacks from time to time. Accept the fact that you may have to flex in response to the little bumps and pivot when you encounter those boulders rolling towards you. We'll talk more about the development of branches (not the kind on a tree) and sequels as you anticipate or actually encounter obstacles in your path on your journey to get through the tumultuous ten.

Fine Tune and Prune Away Mission Creep

Over the years, I've learned that nothing escapes the threat of mission creep. I've grown to accept that it may be hard to detect at first because it's usually a minor change or modification. You yourself may actually be a key contributor to the creep getting into the priorities that you're executing. Sometimes, we change our priorities too quickly based on faulty information that eventually leads us down an unknown path.

Of course, we need to recognize mission creep, but keep note of the things that led you onto the new path because it may be an indicator that you may have to do a full analysis of your priorities and your plans to implement the things you want to do. It's okay to have a strategic pause while you reevaluate, but be mindful of the time you spend on searching through all the forensic evidence that you've gathered. I particularly like to use the lean management techniques of the 5 whys or the root cause diagram as a starting point to help me with determining the origin of the mission creep.

Design and Replicate the Good Stuff

As you design your routine, keep in mind that it's your custom plan, and it's perfectly fine if you occasionally update it to meet all of your needs. Sounds like a no-brainer, but I mention this because sometimes we all have a tendency to start with that "thing" and not want to change it. It may be because we've got so much time in the design (sunk cost) or because we figure that it'll smooth itself out over a period of time.

Consider the story of companies that once had a great product and made lots of money as a result. Some of these companies were seen as titans of their particular industries. They were staffed by some of the smartest people in the world. Yet, over time, these companies faltered and couldn't recover. In many cases, they didn't survive or were purchased for pennies on the dollar. Why? Well, it was because the company executives thought their "mousetrap" would always remain the best. They failed to change with the market. Although this is a strategic level example, you can easily understand the effects of being too rigid.

Study the Routines of Others

As you develop and begin to execute various parts of your powerful routine, you may reach a point where you need a vector check to determine if what you're doing is so radical that it may send you way off course. You may find that you're encountering too much friction and may need to pivot, but you don't have a clear idea of what to do without starting from scratch.

During times like these, you need to benchmark from others. You need reassurance to make sure you're still running along a path that's going forward. It's quite easy to be in a loop wasting energy on the hamster wheel of performance, along with millions of others in the workforce. There are numerous resources available to tap into. As discussed, you should leverage tools to mine the data you need, keeping in mind that you can't expect to get the same exact outcome as others have; you have to customize all routines to meet your needs.

Check Point: Take Inventory

As we're running along our path and making good advances, it can feel a bit uncomfortable to slow down to take account of what we've done and what we need to do. I totally get it, we're cooking and doing great things. In addition, we're doing well addressing all the things on the priority list. Pressing the point further, there's nothing but fair winds and following seas with nary an obstacle you can't avoid.

My message to you is to be wary. Even though things are going well right now, you have to start thinking about the storm that may hit in a few months. So, take inventory of all the priorities you've incorporated into your powerful routine and capture it all so you can replicate the good stuff.

Pre-Plan

You will find that an essential part of building a powerful routine is the initial work involved with pre-planning. Your routine necessitates looking forward into each week ahead of time to conduct pre-planning. This allows you to get a good look at what to expect. This practice takes discipline because you have to bake this into your strategy, and it cannot be omitted. Sure, you'll be having a meeting with yourself, and it might appear a little goofy at first, but this routine is really good training for muscle memory.

In the military, we conducted calendar reviews with senior leaders to ensure everyone was on the same page regarding what was coming down the pike for the week ahead. It was part of our pre-planning strategy. If we were really ambitious, we would look two weeks ahead. Unfortunately, the senior leader calendars changed so frequently that it was a waste of time to look too much farther ahead.

Congratulations! You'll be entering into the next part of the book, focusing on the development of a strong center of gravity. In the next chapter, we'll take a closer look at deliberate planning.

CHAPTER #6

Create a Deliberate Plan

"A goal without a plan is just a wish."

- Antoine de Saint-Exupéry

In 1999, most of the world was preparing for the unknown. No one really knew what was going to happen when the clock struck midnight on 1 January 2000. This global occurrence was called many names, such as: Y2K problem, Y2K scare, Y2K glitch, and millennium bug to name a few. As you know, there were songs and movies about the potential collapse of all that we knew the world to be because the computers might shut down. In the real world, it was really a big, big deal and a tough problem to plan for.

In the months leading up to the year 2000, this concern was shared by many governments all over the world. As a result, the US military created lots of plans that addressed what needed to be done if something bad happened. I was working on the staff of a relatively small organization as a planning and programming officer. By the time January 1999 rolled around, we were in full swing of writing plans for just about every scenario you could think of. Of course, the obvious plans involved the communications infrastructure and all the things controlled by any type of computer interface. Thousands of documents, briefings, and billions of dollars were spent in the United States alone. During this time, I finally began to understand and appreciate the importance of deliberate planning to guide decision making and mitigate potential problems.

Reference Points

In the days before the Global Positioning System (GPS), we relied heavily on maps and reference points to help us reach our destination. Of course, today, maps and reference points aren't used much at all. However, when developing your plan, it's essential that you use a common set of reference points to assist in creating your deliberate plan.

Although reference points may not get you all the way, they get you really close.

Common Frame of Reference

Understanding where your job position fits within the grand scheme of the organization usually begins with a general understanding of the company's purpose for existing. Conceptually, this is aimed at the meaningful pursuits of the company and is viewed as more than producing a profit for the owners or shareholders. The document, or series of documents, is a leadership vetted and approved official statement disseminated throughout the company. It outlines the current state of the company and the desired end state, with documented milestones and measurement areas to support the why and the how of meeting the company plan at a specified time in the future.

As you align your professional goals to be impactful within the organization, use the company vision and mission statements as a common frame of reference when creating the details around your deliberate plan. Extract the important details to help you create and refine the impact you would like to make in the organization. Referencing the mission and vision is especially helpful as a company's vision and mission is usually fixed for a number of years.

The tenets of the vision and mission are normally clearly articulated and should be directly tied to the company's strategic plan or grand strategy. Fortunately, this allows you to draw a direct linkage between what the company views as important and your aspirations to be a successful contributor to achieve success within the organization.

Pursue Objectives

Aligning the attributes of your deliberate plan that includes your goals, professional development desires, and other elements to the company goals and objectives will help guarantee success. First, many people are not devoting this level of detail to producing a deliberate plan to reach their career aspirations. Secondly, this is also a journey of self discovery, so the method you choose to pursue your objectives are distinctly yours.

A common theme you will notice throughout the book is the emphasis for you to start moving forward. You must expend the energy to move forward in pursuit of your goals. This is something no one else can do for you. Although you may harbor a lot of uncertainty about the desired outcome, set your mind at ease, because the tools and techniques that you learn in this book will aid you tremendously.

Lean Into the Challenges Ahead

Leaning into the challenges ahead means accepting the reality that you must do something different to accelerate your career than you have done before. I've talked a bit about seizing opportunities in an earlier chapter that I hope resonated with you. Make note of your surroundings; you will see that people in your organization are throwing their names in the hat for opportunities, working diligently to move up in the ranks, and making an impact in the company. The efforts of those people spur everyone to face their challenge squarely. You must also face challenges with enthusiasm, not disdain, because you have a lot of people working equally as hard to achieve their professional goals and aspirations.

We often get so engrossed in getting to the desired end state that we fail to realize that the sense of fulfillment actually lies in the experience and not the end. Throughout the time you build your plan, implement, and review, you will be in a state of growth. If you execute your growth strategy properly, you will significantly reduce your learning curve by many months.

Plan Your Roadmap to Success

The idea of building a plan from scratch may seem like a daunting task. As you know, the best way to start a plan that will serve as your roadmap to success is to begin with the end in mind. Ask some key questions that prompt you to think deeply. It won't be an easy process, but putting in time to think before putting pen to paper will yield great dividends. What you seek is clarity of purpose regarding your career (and personal) moves for the next year or more of your life.

Here are some key areas to include in your plan:

Current Situation	Evaluation Criteria	Key Evaluation Dates	Challenges
Mission & Vision	Short-Term Goals & Long-Term Goals	Professional Dev Opportunities & Cost	Desired End State
Job Description	Career Progression	Comms Strategy	Lessons Learned

When I created my first plan, I was ambitious and wrote it out to reflect a desired endstate of where I wanted to be in my career after 10 years. Think of your plan as the overarching grand strategy for what you want to do. However, understand that your plan must be a living document; be prepared to review it on a regular basis. As you know by now, I'm a real big fan of pulling out the butcher paper, pens, and sticky notes.

The Plan is Uniquely Yours

Logically, the plan that you create must be uniquely yours. It will include your goals, priorities, and strategy to align with the company vision and mission among other key areas. You should be very detailed; include your best estimate of time frames, different initiatives, key evaluation criteria, etc.

In the previous chapter, I talked about studying the routines of others. Examining the plans of others is not as straightforward because you will usually have to piece together a person's strategy based on a variety of factors. You will need to know information about their key accomplishments, translate the impact of time and environment, draw parallels for today's environment, and include recovery methods used to overcome documented failures.

Eliminate the Noise

As you develop your plan, you will likely encounter self doubt and may question the validity of doing any of the work. Feeling this way is normal because it is a lot of work. Nevertheless, you should press forward with putting the work into developing your plan. Getting on with starting your growth plan is especially critical if you've already tried other methods and just can't seem to get any traction to jumpstart your career. Let that self doubt become your fuel because I believe you will be able to look back at your achievements a year later with a sense of accomplishment and overall pride.

In addition, I think you should return to Chapter 1 of the book and study the key points about why so many people fall into the Being Barely Better Than Others Trap. As with most new things we encounter in our lives, we are sometimes wary of change. If it works better, you can take the incremental steps of spacing your work over a few weeks, but any longer will impact continuity of thought.

Lastly, you have to make sure you don't get overwhelmed by the data gathering process. There's potential for it to be a detail-heavy project. Be careful of having too much information.

If you pack it full of data, you will probably be so happy to announce the mission complete that all your effort will turn into a no hit wonder. You will review the product one time, celebrate finishing the draft, and place it somewhere on your shelf. Strive to make it a usable document.

Set a Start Date

Although you may prefer to set the start date of the deliberate plan to coincide with your evaluation period, I recommend you should start working on it as soon as possible. To clarify, I'm merely referring to when you plan to start crafting your deliberate plan. In fact, you've already begun the growth process by reading this book. At this point, you are pulling data together so you have key elements of a deliberate plan ready to go. It will likely take a few days to incorporate the plan into your preferred software and organize the way you prefer for future review and editing. I know we all agree that your plan should be in the cloud so that it's accessible wherever you have an internet connection. This will give you the flexibility of making updates and creating new parts on the fly as the ideas come to you.

Flexible Planning is the Key

History is replete with examples where flexible planning was the key to success in the face of uncertainty. Certainly, the Lewis and Clark expedition is one of the best examples. The expedition would have failed had it not been for the team's flexible planning as the expedition was deep into the interior of

North America, thousands of miles away from any assistance. Also, think for a moment about another great frontier: space. Can you imagine what could have happened to the Apollo 13 crew? The extraordinary team of NASA personnel and the leading commercial contractors working at Houston's Mission Control Center solved a critical problem after an oxygen tank ruptured midway through the mission. The ensuing problem became a race against time to save the lives of the three crew members aboard.

It's very likely that you won't be faced with the abovementioned life or death problems in the workplace. Nonetheless, you will encounter your own share of situations where flexible planning will be essential. Each problem you face will be unique in its own special way. As with most challenges we discussed, you will develop muscle memory and a knack for using flexible planning when facing difficult challenges.

Anticipate Changes in the Landscape

As we know, change is inevitable. We should always figure change into our deliberate planning. The reality is that it's impossible for any person, company, or government to anticipate all changes in the landscape. The COVID-19 pandemic is a textbook example of a global disruptor that has likely permanently changed many different aspects of our society and business.

At the tactical level, we have to think about the things that are in our immediate circle of influence and one to two levels beyond. Our objective is to make the best of challenging situations and accelerate our understanding of the environment. We must routinely search for indicators of the change. This includes reading external material that has to do with your industry, publicly available annual sales reports, and communications releases. Think of it as taking all these loose pieces of information and using them to create a mosaic that starts from putting those nuggets that leads to a pattern and eventually a picture. Aggregating this information is possible through the use of artificial intelligence data mining tools.

Perfect Conditions Don't Exist

You should never wait for absolutely "perfect" conditions. Perfect will never happen. You will always have some degree of risk that you must accept. We can "buy down" or reduce risk by doing our due diligence through research, surveys, and observation. Yet, that is still not going to be 100% accurate because of the human factor, plus other internal and external pressures.

As discussed earlier, company priorities change, budgets expand and contract, and leaders enter and exit companies. We can probably point to cases where we thought our plan for success was aligned to the mission, vision, and values. Then, we found out something had changed. Perhaps there was a realignment of resources and leadership that caught you off guard. Our goal is to be able to anticipate these changes a lot better than many of our peers and flex to meet the current situation.

Nothing Goes As Planned: Develop Branches and Sequels

One thing is for certain, nothing will ever go as planned. That definitely includes your plans for success. In the military, sometimes when a major plan is created, a Fragmentary Plan (FRAGPLAN) is produced to accompany the overall plan. In the simplest terms, the FRAGPLAN is typically created to address some concern about potential events that might happen that may jeopardize the overall successful execution of the plan. Multiple options built into the base plan are called branches, and the follow-on activities based on the outcome of plans are called sequels.

As you develop your plan, take a bit of time to anticipate several scenarios. Sometimes, just the fact that you have gone through the mechanics of thinking through potential problems will greatly assist you in cases of miscues. Likewise, the news can also be good, as there could be additional funds that unlock a short notice opportunity to a wonderful program that fits perfectly with what you want to do. In any case, you should be ready to quickly work through issues that come your way.

In Chapter 7, we'll continue our study on developing a strong center of gravity. Our discussion will focus on how you can build on these lessons by demonstrating your value like no one else can.

CHAPTER #7

Demonstrate Your Value

"The archer always arrives with arrows in the quiver."

As the officer in command of a transportation squadron based in Alaska, I worked with an outstanding team of heavy equipment mechanics. These mechanics were responsible for keeping the snow removal equipment and fire trucks operational. The harsh winters of Alaska took a tremendous toll on all mechanical equipment. During the mild weather of "summer," we conducted a rebuild and refit of all the snow equipment and fire trucks. The mechanics spent over three months to bring those vehicles back into top shape for the 8 month long "winter," which at times seemed endless.

The snow removable equipment and fire trucks were critical because, without them, the airfield would shut down and all movement on the installation would stop. There were no options to borrow equipment because the nearest major town was 26 miles away in Fairbanks, Alaska. We had to ensure all the repair needs for the vehicles and equipment happened right there on the installation. Although the mechanics were always well respected and admired by me, they earned a greater appreciation from others across the installation as the unrelenting days of the Alaskan winter bore heavily upon us. The mechanics, while small in number, delivered a big impact and truly demonstrated their value each and every day. They performed the herculean task of keeping the equipment operating safely without complaint or fanfare throughout all those cold, dark days. They unabashedly knew we could always rely on them to get the job done.

One of the most important attributes of demonstrating your value is consistency. Although it may seem simple, it can be very elusive to master. Consistent, sustained superior performance is a key discriminator for those wishing to accelerate in the workplace. The perception others have of your value is directly related to you consistently delivering a quality product. It's especially critical when you first join the team to deliver your tasks early when possible and provide meaningful input as you collaborate with others to deliver a product. Although no one may expect you to hit home runs as soon as you arrive, you will be expected to make an immediate contribution.

Craft Your Pitch

Many of us have a hard time talking about our own accomplishments. We enjoy giving all the people on the team credit for their hard work, but we gloss over our own accomplishments. Of course, people respect a person who is humble and believes in giving others recognition. People like this are generally viewed as all-around good people. Please be aware that a good person who never takes credit or expects credit for their hard work is valued but may not be as widely known in the organization as they should be.

At some point, you will need to talk about your professional accomplishments. You must comfortably highlight your successes and articulate the lasting contributions you have made and continue to make in the organization. The pitch is the proven method for conveying your role, top achievements, short-term goals, where you can contribute, and if appropriate, a request for assistance.

Stay Ready: Create and Refine Your Pitch

To be effective, you must be brief, engaging, and clear about your request if ever given the opportunity to say your pitch. A good pitch happens when your professional growth plan and your personal vision converge. Of course, we know that your pitch opportunity won't be as obvious as someone coming up to you requesting to hear your pitch. It will probably occur with someone in a higher position nodding hello or asking you the familiar question of how things are going.

Most of your pitches should conclude with a short request that allows you to build upon this initial conversation. If you're speaking with your supervisor's immediate boss, it may be an invitation for you to provide a briefing that outlines how you're improving a process. If you're speaking with a senior executive, you might ask to get an appointment on their calendar for a 15-minute meeting. In some organizations that have a rigid hierarchy, both of these actions may be frowned upon, so be aware of your environment. Figure out a way to turn a potentially hollow discussion about the weather into something to build a connection. There always seems to be some sort of commonality you can draw from.

If you get that person's permission and are able to get on their calendar, you should go to the meeting with no more than three questions to ask. You should never enter their office with nothing to talk about but the weather. Take their lead with pleasantries, but don't extend that part of the conversation past 2 minutes. You must always be respectful of their time, but be keenly aware of if they want to continue the conversation for a while longer. At the conclusion of the meeting, thank them for meeting with you and send a follow-up email thanking them again for their time. Don't expect another follow-up meeting, but do try to say hello if you see them in the building or maybe if you're early to a video meeting and there are only a few others on the call.

Prepare and Deliver Presentations Often

The primary, surefire way to demonstrate your value is to present information to colleagues and superiors through speaking engagements. This is an absolutely great opportunity to set yourself apart from many of your peers. Some organizations may have so few people willing to speak in front of an audience that you may receive multiple speaking requests per month. In fact, I've heard that up to two-thirds of the population in the U.S. has a fear of public speaking. If you are fearful of public speaking, please join one of the professional speaking organizations. Becoming a great speaker is one of the quickest ways to set you on the right path for accelerated growth.

The use of video calls offers us more opportunities to present than ever before. Take advantage of the chance to present information for professional organizations in which you belong. Aim to present to people from diverse backgrounds who may have interest in topics that also interest you. You should also reach out to some non-profit organizations for opportunities to provide informational briefings to people who may be using the various services the non-profit offers.

Have a routine for preparing and executing your presentation. You should never just go out there and go for it without taking the time to thoroughly study the material, especially if you are speaking face-to-face. Always seek to have a mastery of the knowledge. Just like a well polished briefing will get noticed by your superiors and peers, a poor showing will also get you noticed. If there is a question and answer session afterwards, you must anticipate at least a few of the likely questions and have an answer in mind. Expertly fielding questions also goes a long way and further galvanizes the positive feeling that people have about your presenting abilities.

Learn From All Experiences and Keep Going

Hey, it's a fact of life that you won't nail your pitch or speaking engagement with 100% accuracy all of the time. We all have our days when we're slightly off. I have definitely had my share of horrible speaking engagements that still haunt me to this day. I have a list of 15 talks that I wish I could take away and have do overs of. However, for every one that I want to take back, I probably have ten or more that I would definitely keep. You know, I've learned more from the speeches that I bombed than the ones where I received a standing ovation.

I will continue to talk about retrospectives where you can reflect and chart a path for recovery because that's such an important aspect of getting you to the optimal speed for growth.

With speaking, you will get better as you speak more and more, but you must keep speaking to keep your skills up to par. If you don't speak for a few months, you will find that it will take you a few engagements until you feel comfortable speaking in front of people, even if it is through a video chat. So, you really should keep going, especially if you screw up. You have to get back on that horse and keep riding forward.

Success Doesn't Happen Overnight

Becoming successful isn't easy. In fact, I always put it in the category of very hard to do. It takes a lot of preparation. We sometimes hear about people who seemingly came from nothing and nowhere yet reached success in record time. People talk about the music stars, sports figures, or investment bankers who reach the top of the game or profession within a very short period of time. And we celebrate them. We celebrate because it's a true oddity; they are the unicorns of the business that are often talked about as being mythical creatures.

Although your growth journey will be accelerated, it still won't happen overnight. I believe you know how to put in the work to reap the benefits. There are no short-cuts, but there are more efficient routes. There are many tools that you will have at your fingertips, but you will need to make sure you use the right tools for the job that you need to do.

One of the best things you can do to safeguard yourself from trying to attain everything you want overnight is to develop the routines we talked about in earlier chapters. Chart your success on a growth chart, just as you would measure the growth of a precious child. Cultivate the success you achieve through daily affirmations and create a ritual of celebrating even the smallest of achievements.

Sometimes, we expect to crush it from day one just like the people we hear about on the news, and we get frustrated and our dismay sets us back for days or even months. The pressures of social media may contribute to our feelings of failure before we even have a full grasp of the mountain range we are about to go across. So do yourself a favor and remember that success isn't always instant, but if done right, it's certainly enduring.

Seize the Opportunity

Sometimes, we get an opportunity to do something that we really didn't think we ever would. That's happened to me a few times in my career, and I am very grateful to those people who had the confidence in me to give me a shot. Oftentimes, your opportunity may be a phone call from a semi-panicked person with news that the primary speaker had to drop out. You're probably not the first person they have called; you are the third person. The person sheepishly gives you the details about the 30 minute speaking engagement at X location on X date (which happens to be 3 days from now). You usually have a prescribed topic, and there may or may not be key speaking points that you need to touch on during your speech. You should quickly look through your calendar for any major conflict and say yes to the person on the other end of the phone. It will be an awesome opportunity. Think of it as a way to build capital for future use.

Opportunity Seldom Knocks at the Best Time

One of the most intriguing things about many of the best opportunities is that they are usually fleeting. It's a one off, this week only, one time good deal. There's a well defined, rapidly approaching expiration date. You will usually have a few days or hours to make your decision.

I have lost count of how many of the situations I've had come my way. I couldn't take them all, but I was able to take most of the opportunities I was given. For every three phenomenal opportunities that come your way, two of them will likely come along at the most inopportune times. It seems like fate plays this game whereby the timing is going to always be off by weeks or months. Now, in some cases, you will be forced to say no, because it just won't work. In cases where you have to juggle things around, I recommend that you seriously consider making the timing work to accept the opportunity.

Many times, this opportunity pops up only because others can't do it, as was with several of the speaking engagements I've had before. In addition, the opportunity might be so much work that you will have to sacrifice weekends or a holiday. No matter what, you will likely have to make a decision that won't be a pure win-win. However, when you look back on the experience gained, there will be elements that connect directly to your future success.

Make Calculated Sacrifices

One of the toughest things about pursuing success is that you have to occasionally make sacrifices. Most of the time, the people in our inner circle will understand. Other times, there may be pushback due to a variety of reasons. There may be a few social events you miss because of your commitment to improve. You may have to travel to conferences or events so you stay up to speed with the latest industry trends. Or you may have to step outside your comfort zone a bit to attend the annual office function.

Your job as you execute the plan is to keep those people that you care deeply about informed. You don't have to share all your goals with them, but they should have a reasonable understanding of your "why." Clearly communicating this to your closest allies will likely strengthen your resolve.

Now is not the time to let up off the gas and cruise for a while until something comes along that's easier to do. Sometimes, you will have to get out there and hunt. You will have to take a little more risk by taking on an unfamiliar role because it stretches you to grow more.

Don't Compromise Your Values for an Opportunity

It probably goes without saying that you should not compromise your beliefs or integrity just to have an opportunity to do or participate in something. To put it plainly, this isn't an opportunity; it's a trap. Participating in something that compromises your values will not get you to where you want to go from a career progression standpoint. Aside from the feelings you will have at the time of the "opportunity," you will likely feel so horrible afterwards that you will self-sabotage short-term and maybe long-term opportunities for success that come your way.

There are situations where you may not be fully informed about the event you're participating in and may be in a position where you have very little recourse. In this case, you were likely presented with a bait and switch situation whereby someone gave you bad information about what you were supposed to be doing. So, you end up having to make a decision to continue or stop while you're actively participating in something you don't want to be a part of. Remember, hold rock steady to your values. When a contentious situation arises you will be known more for what you do, than what you said you would do.

Now that you're armed with the tools and techniques provided in Chapters 6 and 7 you're better equipped than ever before to build a strong center of gravity. In Chapter 8, we'll shift our pace into high gear as you learn to move with unflappable confidence as a purposeful leader.

CHAPTER #8

Be a Purposeful Leader

"Every leader walks along the path of uncertainty carrying a vision to share with others."

For every 1,000 leaders that grind it out every day, there are probably 20,000 managers who think of themselves as leaders. Some people don't think of themselves as leaders. They may not be the CEO of a large company, have professional designations before and after their names, or earn a high salary; nonetheless, they are part of the cadre of leaders we aspire to become. The age old debate regarding leaders being born or made still arouses great debates across all spectrums of society. Yet, we all know that no matter what position you take regarding the origins of the great leader, there's a common understanding among all that being a leader is not an easy job.

Throughout the course of my career, I have been fortunate to command at several levels in the Air Force. The standard two year command tour is filled with a lot of daily activity and decisions that must be made in a timely manner. In some cases, you have the luxury of a few days to formulate a solution to a problem. For other decisions, you may sometimes have hours or mere minutes. There's always a team of highly competent professionals working alongside you. You all share the common focus of making the best decisions to keep the mission going as effectively as possible. However, the most difficult decisions are often the ones that affect people. Those are the decisions that you wrestle over, always doing your due diligence to ensure you make the best informed decision possible.

People are the lifeblood of the organization. Therefore, the purposeful leader respects the attributes of each member in the organization. The leader dedicates their time and energy to sharing their vision about how they plan to lead the organization farther. They understand the importance of service and strive to deliver the best version of themself to everyone they encounter.

Incorporate Traits of Great Leaders

We are fortunate to live in our current time for many reasons. One of the things I think about is our access to vast amounts of information on great leaders from the past and present. There is so much material available in print and other media that you can spend countless hours studying, internalizing, identifying unsung heroes, and pulling the best observations from analytical studies of leadership traits in probably every situation imaginable.

So much work has been done to cull down the attributes of great leaders into a distinct number of factors about character, conduct, and overall knowledge. In spite of attempts to place a number on the important attributes and skills required to be a great leader, I believe most people will agree on one thing. All those "things" about a person's ability to lead is underpinned by a desire to constantly grow and be open to change. All the great leaders that I have read about, worked with, or seen in action from afar were constantly stretching themselves and the people around them to reach new heights. These people certainly never let the grass grow between their toes. You're more apt to find them working with many people, making a positive contribution long after "retiring" from their chosen profession.

Study the Experiences of Great Leaders

Create your own leadership laboratory to study the experiences of great leaders. As mentioned, there are tons of resources available. I like to read books about leaders who overcame incredible odds to get to the top of their profession. Another area that you may not have thought about is stepping far outside of your norm to study a person who transformed the entertainment or fashion industry. Usually, if the person is famous, there will be multiple biographies available to read about the leader.

As you study, zero in on the way the leader went about making critical decisions. I particularly enjoy reading autobiographies or viewing firsthand account documentaries. These forms of delivery offer you the insight into what the leader was actually feeling when they encountered the situation or made the big decision.

As with all us humans, nobody is perfect. There's a lot to be learned by someone's mistakes. Therefore, you should also devote time to read about a leader's shortfalls or their unwillingness at times to listen to the wise counsel of those members of their cabinet or organization. If there's a particular thing that's going on in the media involving major figures in society, there are high chances that it will be well documented and available for you to study.

Look Out for Unlikely Leaders

Based on the situation, leaders may seemingly emerge out of the blue. There are many stories related to combat experiences where the most unlikely person is credited with saving the lives of many people all because they saw the urgent need to fill the gap. They might have even started their day as the lowest person in the chain of command, yet they didn't think about that when it was time to act.

In other cases, the unlikely leaders are part of a profession that's neither popular to pursue or well paying, but they may do the job because they are passionate about the craft. I think restaurant cooks and chefs fit into this category. In my college days, I worked at a restaurant for a while and really fell in love with cooking. It's a very satisfying profession, especially when you produce a wonderful meal for others and receive compliments.

Over the years, I dabbled with cooking at home, always joking that one day I would attend a cooking school. So after nearly 30 years of talking about it, I enrolled in cooking school and absolutely loved it. In addition, I met some phenomenal people who were also at home cooks who wanted to kick it up a few notches and shared my passion. We all agreed that the chefs working at the world's best restaurants are also pretty awesome leaders.

Embrace Curiosity: Ask Meaningful Questions

If you're ever given the opportunity to meet a famous leader, try to ask one great question. Don't muddy the question with a long lead in, just ask your question. The sudden, impromptu meetings are difficult because you might be starstruck by the shock of being in the same room. It's a weird thing that's happened to me multiple times. But, if you're at an engagement and you know the person will be answering questions, give it a little thought before you ask the question. Better yet, always have a question ready to go in your head, just in case. Generally, you wouldn't want to stop them from getting on with their day, and you want to always respect their time. The principal may not remember what you did, but the aid, executives, or the executive secretary surely will remember.

If you ever get the opportunity to ask the CEO a question at the company town hall, make sure you keep it at a decently high level. I have seen people ask some pretty specific questions that make the leader do a double take. It presents an uncomfortable atmosphere if you're complaining about toilet tissue not being in the bathrooms on the fifth floor. Remember, use clear and concise communication.

Be a Mindful Observer

One of the best pieces of advice I received early on, that has never failed me, is that successful people are very observant. Even today, I take notice of the environment, i.e., I "read the room" as quickly and as best as I can. I learn the dynamics of what's going on around me and take mental notes. I first learned that lesson prior to entering the Air Force, but I really experienced the importance of being a mindful observer years later as a junior logistics officer.

In the days following 9/11, I deployed with a group of people to conduct aerial support missions in a friendly nation. I was a last minute add-on from a sister unit that had the same training and mission. However, since I wasn't part of the unit that trained together, I had no familiarity with how they executed the mission together as a team. There were some differences, none of them wrong or inappropriate, as to how they operated the team.

Upon arrival, we went straight to work setting up our operations area, tents, and other necessary parts of a base camp. The work was tough, and the weather was non-cooperative some days, but we got everything ready to go. After a few days, the air missions began to arrive, loaded with tons of cargo and troops. As the days turned to weeks, I really felt like part of the team. I contribute this to the fact that I was mindful and respectful of the way their unit personnel went about performing the mission. I was fortunate to have tapped into this highly effective tool of observation and returned home feeling a sense of accomplishment that I had grown from the experience.

Connect with People

In most large organizations, it will be impossible for you to know everyone. Even if you are in an organization with only a few hundred people, it can be challenging. However, you should dedicate some time to connect with people in the organization. Today's telework environment makes it a bit more difficult, but with some work, you can still connect with people. In some ways, it may be easier, because now you're not limited to only knowing and working with people in your immediate area. For example, several months ago I participated in a video call with people from all over the United States, Canada, and even Hong Kong. We each exchanged information at the conclusion of the meeting.

The other key point about connectedness is that you never know who the person may know either directly or indirectly. Whenever I enter an organization, I try to get to know the people I'm working with. This also includes people at all levels throughout the organization. Sometimes, you can learn about people who may be connected to the CEO or other leaders in the organization.

Never underestimate the power of networking. It's probably the most important aspect you can leverage as you work diligently to accelerate quicker than ever before. Networking may offer you early entry into some circles that you might otherwise never be able to enter. Understand that networking is always a reciprocal event. Just as someone may introduce you to a key and influential person, you must also do the same. If you're just getting started, it's sometimes hard to develop that initial set of contacts. I challenge you to get started either building or increasing the network that you already have. Don't make the mistake of thinking that people outside your specific industry won't be able to assist you in some way. It's amazing to think that we're all only about five degrees of connectedness from each other.

Help Others Whenever You Can

Another essential, non-negotiable practice you should follow is to help others whenever you can. To clarify, this is different from putting yourself out there for someone who doesn't care and literally takes advantage of whoever they can. These are not the type of people that I'm referring to helping, unless of course you feel a moral obligation to assist. We help each other so that we can also learn from them; it's reciprocal and the benefits are great.

Helping others is what makes teams cohesive. If you know your co-worker has your back, then you feel great about having their back. This is especially important if you're having a bad day or have to recover from an illness. So, always be on the lookout for how you can help others.

Don't Mistake the Difficult for Being Easy

The idea that a person can drive a car around a track traveling at 180 miles per hour without losing control is amazing to me. The most mind blowing part is that these people, the drivers of super machines, are not on the track alone. They are driving hundreds of miles per hour on an oval race track with dozens of cars packed tightly together, all vying to cross the finish line in first place.

As a casual observer, they make the nearly impossible feat look inviting and sometimes so easy that I think, "Well, I could probably do that." I confidently think to myself, "I drive my car every day, and I've been driving for decades. How hard could it really be?" Then, reality sets in as I see how a small bit of movement, a slight bump among the closely packed race cars, causes unrehearsed, spectacular, super scary accidents. The events happen so quickly that my heart beat goes from resting to "there's a saber tooth tiger chasing me" tempo. Way too fast for a middle-aged person sitting on the couch watching television. In my opinion, these highly talented drivers provide the quintessential example of making something insanely difficult look easy.

Experts Make Tough Tasks Look Easy

As you incorporate stretch goals into your plan, you will likely underestimate how long it will take you to accomplish some of your ambitious goals. Perhaps you have based it on the progression of other people in your organization with a similar background or you benchmark your career progression based on what the CEO of a major corporation might have achieved at the same point in their career some years ago. Nonetheless, you need not worry so much. In fact, you're still on to something good. It's just the fact that these people were so good at what they do that they made it look easy.

Now, at the tactical, everyday level of doing business, one of your goals should be that you become the one who makes the tough tasks look easy to the uninformed. You want to be the expert that your supervisor calls to take care of something that may be giving them wicked fits to solve, but they know that you can calm the storm. Keep in mind that being the person who kills all the big spiders or traps the mice is definitely not what you're shooting for here. Your target is to be so good at something that is valued and really needed in the organization that you're called because you're the one with the juice to avert a crisis.

1. Pull out a drawing pad and a pen for a 5 minute cluster mapping exercise.
2. At the center of the paper, write **Things I Do Well** and draw a line connecting all your ideas around your cluster phrase.
3. Create a list of the top 3-5 items from the map.
4. Incorporate 1-2 things you do into your overall plan.

5. Find opportunities to assist others that need help in areas you do well.

Keep Up with the Pace of the Organization

One of the most crucial areas to accelerate your career is to always keep pace with the organization. This means you have to go where the operations tempo leads you. If the standard is to work a 70-hour work week, you have very little chance of working 40 hours and earning the respect of your peers; quite the opposite will occur. You have to put in 70 hours. Let's face it, working in some organizations is just a grind. The tempo is always super fast, and you have no time to even spend your paycheck. If you're in one of those careers, keep doing great things, but start working on your exit strategy if you know that type of pace isn't conducive to you.

The pace can sometimes ebb and flow based on seasonal change, market conditions, or many other varieties. If you can plot these surges and create some predictability, it will help you adjust things such as professional development opportunities to line up with a lull in the pace so maybe you can get a better chance at the company sending you to the development opportunity. Although everyone may feel certain pressures, this technique may be able to provide a bit of insulation from the churn of highs and lows associated with feast or famine situations regarding the pace of work.

Perhaps you're reading this book because you're seeking the tools that will enable you to transition into or out of a job that's very stressful. Or maybe you're getting a start in an industry that doesn't serve the market you want to serve. In short, there are a lot of reasons why you picked up this book about accelerating your career. All of these reasons are valid. These tools and techniques are cross cutting and deliver information that transcends many industries.

CHAPTER #9

Evaluate and Reflect

"Follow effective action with quiet reflection. From the quiet reflection will come even more effective action."
                                                                    - Peter F. Drucker

---

E arly in my career, I worked closely with Army logistics officers. Even today, I still joke around with my Air Force buddies that I probably should have become an Army logistics officer. I was always impressed by the way they planned, executed, and evaluated military operations. They conducted a thorough analysis with extreme professionalism and built very detailed slides that stepped their leadership through the entire after action review where oftentimes only a few follow-up questions were fielded. Sometimes, it was like listening to an alphabet soup of acronyms and shorthand terms, but I usually left the meetings with deep respect and admiration. Those meetings gave me many ideas about how to visually represent the identification and resolution of complex problems.

This desire for visuals to help me solve problems led to my discovery and routine use of many tools and techniques. When I first joined the Air Force, Total Quality Management was very big, along with Six Sigma, Theory of Constraints, and other lean practices. Over the subsequent years, the military has gone through another handful of tools and techniques that now incorporate agile methodologies. In all cases, the evolution I witnessed during my career has allowed the military to be great at evaluating and reflecting consistently better as time moves on.

Be the Best Version of Yourself

Being the best version of yourself doesn't mean perfect. In fact, it's the opposite. The hope is that you're going to realize your shortfalls and limitations and be able to walk into a room as your authentic self. At times, you will feel outside your depth of knowledge and experience; you will be at your most vulnerable. Those will be the times when you will grow the most. It's what I refer to as the "3:00 a.m. Oh Crap" moments when you're most truthful to yourself. It's also when you should whisper words of encouragement to yourself.

Sometimes, we can feel overwhelmed by our own thoughts. We retreat within ourselves and maybe deny the positive insights that can come through self reflection. I've found that there's often a thin line between self improvement and self deprivation. Don't revisit the bad without also revisiting the good.

Throughout this process, you will be keeping up a tremendous pace. The pressures of daily life won't diminish; they may actually increase for a while. So, through all the ups and downs that you will experience, take the time to give yourself some grace. Pause to take in the moment. Smile more often than you're used to doing and make sure you get a good laugh each day.

Positivity is very important; make it part of your lifeforce. It will allow you to have the energy you need to tackle the bigger challenges ahead. I remember one day while working in the Pentagon, during a particularly tough time, a colleague pulled me to the side. He told me that I was too cheerful. He didn't say it to make me angry or to be a mean person. He told me this because he wanted me to succeed. At the time, I thought it was the craziest thing for a person to say, but after walking through the hallways later that afternoon, I knew exactly what he meant. During my walk, I saw many people going about their day. Each one was on a particular mission. Some were walking with others and some were walking alone. For as many people I saw walking the halls, I didn't see a single person with a smile on their face. It was a pretty dismal place.

Even after his sage advice, I just couldn't stop saying hello with a smile. Maybe it's my Southern roots, but I always tried to greet people and interact with a smile. Over time, it became part of my brand so much so that it allowed me to strike up conversations with people in the Pentagon who I probably wouldn't know today if I had let the weight of "the building" thrust me away from being my authentic self and continuing my journey to be better at all I do.

Solicit Feedback from People You Trust

One of the toughest lessons that I learned years ago is that you should solicit feedback only from people you trust. This is especially true if you want to keep your moves for potential advancement very close-hold. Although we like to think of jealousy as being solely reserved for juveniles, there are adults who haven't evolved in this area of their social development. Instead of a clap of support, they would rather you fell on your face.

The fact is that you can cast your request for feedback wide, across an entire network, but the best feedback will come from the people that you trust. For many years, I kept a very low profile on social media because there are mean spirited people who will offer you nothing but negativity. Unfortunately, there are many people who hide behind their online personas and sling very harsh criticisms without blinking an eye.

Always solicit feedback with a few open-ended questions that can help you improve. I usually ask for feedback after my speaking engagements. Some of my favorites are open-ended questions like those listed below.

How did I do?
How could you tell I was prepared for the presentation?
What is the one thing you believe I can do better?

The answers to these three simple questions will help you make incremental steps for improvement. Receive it with open arms, even though it may be a bit raw; it was likely delivered with care. Once received, it's up to you; allow this newfound information to help you overcome challenges, and it will spur growth.

Document Your Lessons Learned

Although the old phrase "once bitten, twice shy" is often used, the reality is that the likelihood of a human making the same mistake is very high. I understand that this may seem very basic, but it's definitely worth mentioning. Typically, we jot down our notes and maybe look over them once or twice, telling ourselves that we've internalized the findings or problems enough to move onward. We often believe that once we correct an issue we won't make the same mistake twice or have the same miscue. Then, after a few months, we forget.

When you create your system, try to keep it simple so that it's manageable. You also want a product and database that's searchable. I have friends who keep everything on a portable, electronic tablet. It beats the heck out of trying to keep physical notebooks. Documenting will take some time to do, but after you have developed a good template, you will get to the heart of the matter in your write up. Listed below are several prompts that should help you create your lessons learned:

Overview of the event (1-2 lines)	Your role in the event
What went well?	What went badly?
Was it widely attended? Why or why not?	Any applicable metrics?
How could have you made the event better?	Did you have enough organizational support for the event (resources)?

Are post-event surveys available?	If you could change one thing, what would it be?

Recording lessons learned will greatly assist in providing yet another piece of the mosaic that I talked about in previous chapters. By now, identifying and storing information that will make you better should be second nature. You're accelerating your pace with unflappable confidence and in stride to achieve the speed you need. The next thing to do is push yourself even more.

Big Goals

When we are very young, mostly every goal we have starts out as a big goal. You may have told your family and friends that you wanted to become the President of the United States, maybe an astronaut, or a world-renowned doctor. The beautiful thing is that you believed it. The buddies you hung around also had big goals, and they shared them with everyone that would listen, too. You all were in good company. Then, somewhere along the way, you let that big goal slip away from your sights, and your friends let theirs slip away, too. Over time, you stopped talking about it, stopped working towards it, and stopped believing it. Now, it's time to jumpstart the goal-oriented part of you that's been inside all along.

Throughout the book, we've talked about setting goals and measuring your progress as you move forward with accelerating your career. As with all growth, you must routinely establish new goals. Now, you need to dream bigger than ever before. Craft your three stretch goals. These goals are the big scary ones that seem so huge that you aren't comfortable sharing them with someone without laughing. These goals all share a common trait: they may be big and bodacious, but not impossible to achieve. Yes, those are the goals you need to create.

Follow Through

For years, the game of golf was a very difficult sport for me to participate in with any level of competitiveness. I used to make contact with the ball, but it never went much further than 100 yards. I had no idea if the ball would go straight, sideways, or just straight up in the air. So, I went out and bought new shoes, better clubs, and golf clothes. Although I was packaged right and looked the part, I still couldn't play well. It made no difference.

After one particularly rough day on the course, I stumbled back to the clubhouse with hurting feet and a crushed ego. Sitting there along the side of the beverage counter was the club's golf pro hanging up a flier about golf lessons. You see, over the many weeks that I had been out playing golf, it never occurred to me that I needed to take golf lessons. I signed up for the course, and one of the first things we worked on was my follow through. It turns out that I was raising my head up before actually hitting the ball, and my overall swing was choppy. Over the course of just a few days, I learned how to swing with a good follow through, and I began hitting the ball much farther and straighter. That was my first lesson about the power of having a good follow through.

In business, following through refers to going the extra mile to make sure everything is done correctly. Whenever you say you're going to accomplish a goal or task, you need to do it to the best of your ability. If you say you're going to support someone, then support them. Go all the way through until the end. Your value is going to increase within the organization because people will know that you always follow through by being where you say you will be and doing what you say you will do. Organization leaders have two lists. The first list has the people on it that they know will get the job done right, will stay committed to the end, and will have their backs throughout; that list is short. The second (and much longer) list is composed of the people whom they have questions about commitment, quality of work, and focus. Of course, you want to be on the short list.

Crack the Code

I used to think that I had to crack some kind of code to enter into the select group of trusted advisors that surround organizational leaders. However, I found out that, many times, these leaders are simply looking for a group of people they can trust to get the job done correctly, on time, and within budget. They look for people who can consistently replicate their great performance. There aren't many people who can do this, and that's why the circle is small.

There are gatekeepers who guard the door of entry into the world of the senior executive leaders, but great leaders are always on the lookout for great talent. They know that these hardworking, dedicated personnel who produce outstanding work every day are the lifeblood of the company.

Hone Your Skill Set

Every once in a while, we discover a natural ability that others may struggle with. However, you can't rely on raw talent alone. Your commitment to embark on the mission to accelerate your progress will require more than raw talent and the brute of willpower. It's obvious that you're already someone who is highly motivated to get things done, and you don't wait around for a handout. In fact, you feel your best when you have an opportunity to seize the day.

Your future success relies on your continued efforts to get better each day. I think of this as developing your superpower. You're not just trying to be Barely Better Than Others in hopes that you'll easily turn the tide and overcome any challenges based on sheer luck. In just a few weeks, you will complete all the necessary parts of your plan. You know that being in control of your destiny is a wonderful thing. You also understand that life is more than working hard to earn a decent wage, pay your bills, and make sacrifices of your time. In other words, you don't want your career to drive you to the point of missing out on being with the people that you care about.

If you continue to get noticed, you'll be identified, by name and face, as having a specially cultivated skill set so important that you will get the recognition you deserve. I've identified six ways that you can continue to test and train your critical thinking skills in order to bolster your rapid progression while continuing to navigate your way through the tumultuous ten.

- Professional Development
- Case Studies
- Scenario-Based Gaming

- Lessons Learned Archives
- Audit Reports
- Volunteer Your Services

Professional Development

There are numerous professional development organizations that offer web-based training. It's definitely worth the expense you pay to belong to a professional organization. Once you become a member, you have access to hundreds of webinars and the opportunity to attend low-cost social events in your area. I'm a member of several organizations and routinely participate in webinars and social events. In addition, many of the major social media platforms host events that are absolutely free. I encourage you all to subscribe to feeds that send out this information to followers.

Case Studies

You probably studied case studies in college business classes. The nearly two-hundred-year-old case study method is still an effective way to think through hard problems that companies have to solve each day. There are literally thousands of case studies available that cover a wide range of topics and scenarios that will test your skill set. I recommend you study at least one per month. I believe it's a small investment in your time that will pay off in improving your critical thinking skills.

Scenario-Based Gaming

I want to highlight and give credit to the awesome designers of simulations. At this point, you can probably find the online gaming software download for many scenarios. The level of detail is impressive, and many of the games are very popular. These games replicate real-world scenarios and incorporate a myriad of options the gamer may choose from in real-time. These online games also allow you to play with multiple players from around the world and rely heavily on collaborative, complex problem solving. They can significantly bolster your critical thinking skills and help you formulate better solutions when faced with real-world problems.

Lessons Learned Archives

Many companies have internal lessons learned in their shared archives site. In my opinion, these provide an excellent source of materials and knowledge that is unmatched. Sorting through the library can be tedious if there isn't a standardized records management system for archiving. Often, the information is security protected, so you will need to get special permission, and in some cases, you will have to have a "need to know." However, it will probably be well worth the effort to gain access to this treasure trove of valuable information.

Audit Reports

Although audits aren't a glamorous part of the business, they do offer keen insights. In this case, I'm referring to process audits, not financial audits or annual financials. You will likely find many more reports if you work in the government sector. Typically, there are rules in place requiring these reports be on file for a number of years after the audit was concluded. In some cases, audit follow-up actions are ongoing for many years into the future. In fact, your company may have an entire compliance area. Again, you may be limited by your "need to know" status.

Volunteer Your Services

Lastly, I included volunteerism as an ideal way to test your skills because it serves a twofold purpose. First, you're helping people and contributing positively to your community. You will immediately see the impact of your efforts. Secondly, I know that you all want to put your best foot forward in all that you do. It doesn't matter if you're getting paid or not. Your satisfaction lies in consistently doing things right because it's in your nature. I'm sure any organization would love to have you volunteer your time and provide your unmatched expertise.

We've covered a lot of ground over these past nine chapters. My intent is to show you how to get through the churn of the tumultuous ten months that it would have taken you to get to a higher level of knowledge and start making an impact sooner than you have ever before.

You have the foundational attribute needed for proper growth: a strong and powerful center of gravity. You have attained knowledge of the elements you need for an actionable, deliberate plan and the guiding north star attributes for a strong value. With all that you know now, you're well on your way to accelerating your pace with unflappable confidence.

In Chapter 10, we'll talk about the final tools you need to pull everything together. You will overcome the learning curve and be so effective that it will surprise you. So, let's continue onward to our mission objective with **boldness, brilliance,** and **benevolence**.

CHAPTER #10

Convergence

"Learning is like rowing upstream – not to advance is to drop back."

- Chinese proverb

The perfect example of convergence is the preparation of a delicious meal. First, you must create a menu based on your environment: the season, the tastes of the guests, the limitations of your kitchen, etc. Next, you source all the recipes and realistically determine how much time you have to prepare the meal. Then, you must acquire all the supplies you need to create a wonderful experience.

Long before the first guest arrives, you do all of your prepping. You set up the proper mise en place to guarantee that all ingredients are at your cooking station. Each component has a purpose to bring out a distinct flavor in the meal. In fact, you may spend over half of your cooking experience at the prep station. When the time is right, you follow the recipes for the sake of consistency and put your heart into creating the absolute closest thing possible to perfection. Your feedback is nearly immediate as you see the smiles and nodding heads of approval from all of your guests. This is where science and art meet to yield fantastic results.

Solutions

At the beginning of this book, I promised to provide you with the tools and techniques you need in order to accelerate your career. Your problem statement was: What should I do? **There's a steep learning curve, I have little to no time to get up to speed, and I want to be an effective, valued member of the team ASAP.** The solution you seek is my recipe to overcome the tumultuous ten. It's a blueprint based on six principal things you can do in order to accelerate your career:

- Communicate Clearly
- Build a Powerful Routine
- Create a Deliberate Plan
- Demonstrate Your Value
- Be a Purposeful Leader
- Evaluate and Reflect

These principal areas provide the strategic overview you need. See below for specific lesson topics that provide additional clarity.

- Overcoming **B**eing **B**arely **B**etter **T**han **O**thers (3BTO)
- Leveraging Evaluations
- Developing Your Performance Plan

- Understanding Tasks
- Delivering Accurate Reports
- Recovering from Miscues
- Connecting with Others
- Eliminating Wasteful Habits
- Prioritizing
- Best Practices
- Critical Components of a Deliberate Plan
- Crafting Your Personal Pitch
- Taking Charge of Your Destiny
- Studying Great Leaders
- Staying Proficient
- Becoming the Best Version of Yourself

Think of the areas as guideposts *to aid you on your journey to achieve* extraordinary success.

Staying Power

At some point in the near future, you will begin to check off your goals and add more things you want to accomplish. In Chapter 9, we talked about honing your skill set through routine experiences designed to immerse you in solving complex problems. This is especially crucial as you take on additional opportunities and responsibilities in the organization.

As with many things in life, the key to getting better is consistently doing things the right way. The toughest part about being in the business environment is that every scenario you will face is just a little bit different. However, you will notice that there are many similarities. Also, leverage the expertise of the people in your trusted circle to assist you in testing out new strategies and techniques for identifying and solving problems.

Throughout your journey, remain confident in your abilities to solve complex problems and contribute positively to the organization. You must remain patient with yourself and be keenly aware that you won't be perfect in everything you do. No one is able to sustain flawless performance; if you stumble, you will have the tools to get back on track. Write about your experiences in the safe spaces of your journal. Trust and grace are the watchwords for recovery.

Words to the Wise

Celebrate the small victories and major triumphs alike. Although your pace will at times be grueling, you can pause to reflect on your good fortune. You will know that it wasn't luck that gave you an unexpected gift; it was your hard work. Include those close to you in your celebrations. They were probably part of the reason why you accomplished your feat.

Once the word spreads that you produce outstanding work in a timely manner, expect the notoriety to come with certain unspoken commitments. Your reward will likely be more work. This is especially true if you're working in a salaried position. If you work a lot with clients, make yourself indispensable to them as well. They will appreciate the skills you have and will likely put you on their unofficial list of people they enjoy working with.

I also recommend that you work on developing your interpersonal skills. You will interact with people from other areas in the company and in the local chapters of the professional organizations. So, you will begin to see some parts of your growth and training plan change. Although it might appear to be mission creep, try to think with a long term mentality.

Remember to seek the help of others as you traverse unfamiliar areas. This is a reciprocal effort; be prepared to assist those that assist you. Always try to seek help well before it's crunch time. The person or people will greatly appreciate not having to drop everything they are doing to assist or guide you through a task.

Lastly, embrace the requests to mentor and train others. This is not only an excellent way to show additional value, but it will be a fantastic networking opportunity. As I said numerous times throughout the book, the people in any organization are the lifeblood.

Final Thoughts

Just like the cooking example at the beginning of the chapter, there is an element of art and science involved in becoming a successful leader. The art is oftentimes attributed with the people skills one must master in order to attract and retain the best workforce, whereas the science is the measurements, metrics, budgets, and projections. Of course, I've seen the blurred lines throughout my career as an Air Force officer.

Although you will never enter in any pursuit blindly, you must take calculated risks along the way. Understand that nothing is 100% either way. Many times, you have to make the decisions with the best possible answers you have at the time. You have the confidence you need, the tools to accomplish your mission, and the roadmap that shows the best route to reach your destination. So, now is the time to move out and reach the summit of your success. Press onward with **Boldness, Brilliance,** and **Benevolence.**

Thank you all very much for reading my book. My wish is that this book changes you in a profound and remarkable way. I have distilled the most potent version of life learned lessons to give you the tools and techniques needed to significantly reduce your learning curve at any new job or position. I want you to accelerate your career like never before and succeed beyond your wildest dreams. Please contact me at: marktate@ transcendentconsultingllc.com or visit transcendentconsultingllc. com for the latest blogs and information or to schedule a session or take part in future live-streamed events.

CONCLUSION

The warm summer sun was bright as I stepped outside to get into my truck. The day was very emotional. Moments earlier, I had given my final salute during my retirement ceremony. Now, after being affiliated with the military for over 32 years, first as a cadet in the Reserve Officer Training Corps while at Auburn University, then serving on active duty for over 27 years, it was time for me to take off the uniform for good.

I'd experienced a lot in between my commissioning ceremony and my retirement ceremony after serving all those years of active duty. Along the way, I'd lost relatives, friends, and colleagues, far too many people to think about without my eyes becoming moist. My mental contact list was overflowing with the names and faces of hundreds, if not thousands of people I'd met and known throughout my service. I felt happiness for my family, friends, colleagues, and myself. I had a lot of assistance getting to this point in my military career. Many of my relatives traveled out to Utah for the retirement ceremony, shocking me because I figured there would be only a handful to witness the event.

But, to my surprise, there were so many relatives that there was a whole section just for them. We were South Carolina and Alabama strong.

In the weeks that followed my retirement, I came up with an idea for a book that could teach people how to operate and thrive in high pressure, competitive environments. I always seemed to make up excuses as to why I wouldn't be able to write a book. One day, I woke up, and my eyes locked on a quote that I've had for many years from Socrates that says, "Let him that would move the world first move himself." I guess something clicked, and during the following weeks, I wrote the rough manuscript with a person like you in mind.

Why Taking Action Is Important

Acting on the lessons in this book will allow you to learn and perform at a higher level than ever before. I would like you to break away from running with a tight gaggle of peers and lead the pack. There's such a different view when you're running out front. Remember, time waits for no one, and if you wait too long, you might wake up feeling that time has passed you a long time ago.

This is your opportunity to face whatever your reality is today and change the narrative into whatever you want the story to become. The universe wants you to shift because you're reading this book. If you've gotten this far, then you have something burning inside that is ready to face the future with **boldness**, **brilliance**, and **benevolence**. So, shatter the old paradigms. You don't need to spend a vast amount of time to reach the level where you're an impact player in your organization. With these tools and techniques, you can get on the path of greatness and become an impactful leader quickly, efficiently, and effectively. As they say: you drive the car, don't let the car drive you!

What Your Better Future Looks Like

There's a story about a young man named Mark from Spartanburg, South Carolina who worked hard in the scorching heat of the Carolina sun to save up money for college. Although far from being a middle class kid, his parents raised him well and took care to provide the tools he needed to achieve success. They emphasized integrity, drive, boldness, and benevolence. He was fortunate that both parents thought of education as the key to unlock many doors. Short-term sacrifices for long-term gain was the mantra shared throughout the household. The true measure of success was not how each skirmish was fought, but how one overcame the unsettling blows and barriers in life that sometimes impeded the path of achievement.

He battled through college for over five years, experiencing the ups and downs that go along with life. At one point, he thought for a few minutes about packing it all up and heading back home, but he quickly recovered and retooled. He dug in and fought on with encouragement from family and friends. It was a hard fought battle, but he won, becoming only one of a handful in his extended family with a college degree. And when he graduated, he was optimistic that the days ahead would be much brighter.

Then, he faced more tribulations while in the military. There were some missteps along the way, but he took note, made corrections, and moved forward. Eventually, over the course of years, he came across his own version of lightning in a bottle. This knowledge became a game changer, and just like the small sapling that turns into the giant oak, he began to achieve success beyond what many thought possible. And now he's just hit stride and is running in full sprint mode, getting it done with **boldness**, **brilliance**, and **benevolence**.

Now, let's talk about what your better future looks like. Imagine that you've accomplished the top 10 goals you set and are now moving onward to the others. People ask, "How were you able to overcome the challenges of a steep learning curve and demanding schedule to become impactful in the organization so rapidly?" You smile within because what they ask is based on the absolute truth. It's true, you are performing at a high level, and you've crushed your goal of being impactful in your organization well ahead of your own plans.

All the leadership in the organization know who you are and have promoted you for the fifth time in three years. You are a recognized expert and you enjoy helping people. You're a difference maker who shares your knowledge willingly. As a result, you have opportunities that you never dreamed you would ever have. You've already cut your teeth leading some big projects and have become one of a few company intrapreneurs. So, after only a relatively short time, people have begun to anticipate that your transition to becoming a successful entrepreneur is inevitable.

Not only are you thriving professionally, but socially as well. You have a wonderful, dependable group of caring people in your circle. All parties assist each other in whatever way they can. You can freely bounce ideas off of your colleagues. They give you candid feedback that is well thought and deliver it constructively with respect and care. You are pleased with your performance and have a clear plan for what you want to do in the future. You've made it to the other side to the bigger, better future that you've always dreamed of, and it feels very, very good.

If You Fail to Act

If you don't use this book to help you, the status quo remains in place. You will miss out on the opportunity to change your situation. Perhaps you have been contemplating a change, but you were too nervous or too timid to act. Maybe you will level with yourself on the fact that you're not living up to your potential, but you still do nothing. Perhaps those closest to you shake their heads and roll their eyes in utter disappointment because they see so much wasted potential. The tell-tale sign is when they announce your arrival at gatherings before you enter the room, which means for everyone to stop the chatter about your self-imposed shortcomings.

If you fail to act, you will continue to rely on luck and timing to get you a meager annual pay raise that will help pay for the continuance of a bad habit. You will continue job hopping because you'll always be searching for the perfect job where people appreciate what you do. Yet, you won't look squarely in the mirror and begin to appreciate yourself. Success will be elusive, and receiving kudos from others will be as infrequent as an inch of snowfall in Death Valley. Worst yet is that you will be stuck in the phantom comfort zone that's created when you operate with the **B**eing **B**arely **B**etter **T**han **O**thers (3BTO) mentality. I know you can get out of this situation and move forward in my direction. Let me guide you to the path away from this stalking cheetah called failure and get to the protective barrier that hope and success offers.

Final Thoughts

There's a lot of noise in our world today. We are constantly barraged with the latest craze that product X will be the ultimate solution to create a better version of ourselves. Yet, as trends come and go, there is no substitute for good old fashioned hard work. You must direct energy into developing a sturdy foundation, work hard to build the muscle memory required to create a strong center of gravity, and have an unrelenting commitment to pursuing your ambition with unflappable confidence. You need to have the kind of internal confidence where you write the impossible dream on your vision board, create a deliberate plan that outlines how you're going to make it a reality, then pull out all the stops to reach the goal.

Friends, success does not have to be a fleeting event whereby you're happy to experience it but have no idea what you did to make it happen. We don't have to relinquish our destiny to the fate of a spin on the wheel of life in hopes that the spinner will randomly land on the best, most optimal situation for your success. I want you to be so deliberate in your planning, strategy, and self confidence that you shatter all timelines for accomplishing your goals. When the day comes, I want you to look back at your career with happiness and a sense of accomplishment for all the wonderful things you achieved and all the wonderful people you've encountered along the way. Avoid the noise, focus on your mission, and treat yourself and others with respect so we can meet at the mountaintop. Until then, go with peace, happiness, and unbridled optimism for the better years ahead.

ABOUT THE AUTHOR

Colonel (Ret.) Mark E. Tate is the owner of Transcendent Consulting, LLC, a leadership coaching, strategic planning, and facilitation company located in Loudoun County, Virginia. He is a native of Spartanburg, South Carolina and is a graduate of Auburn University, Alabama. Mark earned his commission through the Air Force Reserve Officer Training Corps while attending Auburn University. During his 27 years of military service, he served as a Logistics Readiness Officer in a variety of positions spanning seventeen assignments and deployments. Mark commanded organizations on three occasions, served as a staff officer in multiple combatant commands, took part in contingency deployments, and was selected for various duty assignments throughout the world. He and his wife, Dedra, live in Northern Virginia with their three daughters.

In his youthful days, Mark worked as a salesperson at his father's produce and fruit stand. He fondly remembers the days when he worked with his dad during every summer month of his high school and college years. He found it extremely rewarding to see the satisfied smiles on customers faces. After retiring from the military, Mark was encouraged by his spouse to participate in the Dog Tag Fellowship Program hosted by the Dog Tag Bakery in Washington, District of Columbia. This non-profit entrepreneurial jumpstart program for veterans, military spouses and caregivers was the perfect catalyst he needed to start his consulting business. He founded Transcendent Consulting, LLC to provide clients with the tools and techniques they need to reduce risk, manage efficiency, and approach problems in a more flexible and dynamic way.

www.ingramcontent.com/pod-product-compliance
Lightning Source LLC
Chambersburg PA
CBHW060612200326
41521CB00007B/746